BUSINESS ISSUES, COMPETITION AND ENTREPRENEURSHIP

T0291388

PRIVATE EQUITY GLOBALISATION

ETHICAL BUSINESS CHALLENGES

BUSINESS ISSUES, COMPETITION
AND ENTREPRENEURSHIP

Additional books and e-books in this series can be found on Nova's website under the Series tab.

BUSINESS ISSUES, COMPETITION AND ENTREPRENEURSHIP

PRIVATE EQUITY GLOBALISATION

ETHICAL BUSINESS CHALLENGES

MARIA ALEJANDRA MADI

nova
science publishers
New York

NOTICE TO THE READER

The Publisher has taken reasonable care in the preparation of this book, but makes no expressed or implied warranty of any kind and assumes no responsibility for any errors or omissions. No liability is assumed for incidental or consequential damages in connection with or arising out of information contained in this book. The Publisher shall not be liable for any special, consequential, or exemplary damages resulting, in whole or in part, from the readers' use of, or reliance upon, this material. Any parts of this book based on government reports are so indicated and copyright is claimed for those parts to the extent applicable to compilations of such works.

Independent verification should be sought for any data, advice or recommendations contained in this book. In addition, no responsibility is assumed by the publisher for any injury and/or damage to persons or property arising from any methods, products, instructions, ideas or otherwise contained in this publication.

This publication is designed to provide accurate and authoritative information with regard to the subject matter covered herein. It is sold with the clear understanding that the Publisher is not engaged in rendering legal or any other professional services. If legal or any other expert assistance is required, the services of a competent person should be sought. FROM A DECLARATION OF PARTICIPANTS JOINTLY ADOPTED BY A COMMITTEE OF THE AMERICAN BAR ASSOCIATION AND A COMMITTEE OF PUBLISHERS.

Additional color graphics may be available in the e-book version of this book.

Library of Congress Cataloging-in-Publication Data

Names: Madi, Maria Alejandra, author.
Title: Private equity globalisation: ethical business challenges / Maria
Alejandra Madi (UNICAMP, Brazil; The Green Economics Institute, UK).
Description: Hauppauge, NY: Nova Science Publishers, Inc., [2019] | Series:
Business issues, competition and entrepreneurship | Includes bibliographical references and index.
Identifiers: LCCN 2019012346 (print) | LCCN 2019014298 (ebook) | ISBN
9781536153064 () | ISBN 9781536150438 (softcover)
Subjects: LCSH: Private equity. | Business ethics.
Classification: LCC HG4751 (ebook) | LCC HG4751 .C3637 2019 (print) | DDC 174/.4--dc23
LC record available at https://lccn.loc.gov/2019012346

Published by Nova Science Publishers, Inc. † New York

CONTENTS

PREFACE

This book aims to fill a gap in existing literature in order to contribute to the understanding of the main features and outcomes of the private equity business model that has already been spread around the world. Private equity funds have been drivers of the financialisation of the global economy. Lying at the juncture of the real economy and the shadow banking system, private equity funds draw upon capital and debt to acquire stakes in companies that are intended to be sold for profit after a number of years. Indeed, these institutional investors have a key role in the diversification of global investments. Although US private equity firms are still dominant, the global private equity industry has been mainly moving towards Europe and the Asia-Pacific region.

The process of financialisation has contributed to unprecedented social, political, and environmental challenges. In this setting, the complexity of social and economic policy problems of the 21st century requires the recognition of the role of private equity globalization in the selection of investments and in the creation of new business structures. The shifts in corporate ownership, trough waves of mergers and acquisitions, have created new business structures where companies are considered bundles of assets and liabilities to be traded in order to get short-term returns. Indeed, new investment and portfolio management practices have been overwhelmed by the financialisation of wealth and "short-termism" in American and European business. While private equity investors aim to maximize their short-term returns, private equity funds turn to be major transnational employers.

The outcomes of the global financial crisis of 2007-2008 made clear the need to redress and redesign business models and re-balance corporate power in order to broaden the dialogue on social responsibility. Maria Alejandra Madi's book aims to foster a deeper understanding of the ethical challenges related to the private equity financial engineering model. In short, the book aims to prepare the reader for participating in a fruitful debate. The main target is the transformation of the global economy to a more just and sustainable one.

This book is recommended for a broad interdisciplinary audience. Not only students in economics, management and international business, but also policy makers, regulators, managers and investors. Reading this book will benefit all those who seek to better understand the complex stakes in the evolution of the capitalist system, in the tensions between short-term profit targets, regulatory policies, and participatory openings in governance and social inclusion.

INTRODUCTION

This book aims to fill the gap in the existing literature in order to contribute to the understanding of the main features and outcomes of the private equity business model that has recently been spread around the world. Private equity funds have been key actors in the financialisation of the global economy with deep effects on labour and countries. Lying at the juncture of the real economy and the financial economy, private equity funds draw upon capital and debt to acquire stakes in companies that are intended to be sold for profit after a number of years. Indeed, these institutional investors have a key role in the diversification of global investments. Although US private equity firms are still dominant, the private equity industry has mainly moved toward Europe and Asia-Pacific.

The term "private equity" encompasses financial techniques aimed to finance investment in companies. In particular, private equity funds centralize endowments from banks, institutional investors – also pension funds – and high net worth individuals, in order to assume a key – role in the dynamic of investment buyouts of high profit potential. Indeed, the centralization of global capital stimulated the reorganization of financial and productive structures where private equity funds have historically focused on short-term returns instead of building a long-term sustainable business and social environment. Part I addresses the relevance of the Pragmatist ethical approach to business where habits of belief play a relevant role in shaping institutions and their outcomes in society.

Part II discusses the factors that shape the microeconomic and macroeconomic features of the typical and innovative investment strategies. We highlight that the private equity expansion involves social relations driven by profit and competition in a context characterized by increasing economic inequality challenges. While the process of financialisation enhanced the redistribution of power and wealth, the dynamics of the private equity business model arose ethical concerns. The financial engineering strategies and practices of private equity funds have historically been, in truth, mechanisms that promote the expansion of the global financial markets. Today, private equity funds express the power of centralized money to define not only investment flows but also working conditions. In this scenario, private equity funds emerged as major transnational employers. They are also responsible for the employment standards of tens of millions of workers worldwide.

The transformations in corporate ownership, trough waves of mergers and acquisitions, have created a new business structure – the private equity business structure- where companies are managed as bundles of assets and liabilities to be traded in order to get short-term returns. Indeed, the private equity investment and management practices have been overwhelmed by the financialisation of wealth that reinforced "short-termism" in American and European business. The globalization of capital has contributed to unprecedented social, economic and environmental challenges. The global financial crisis of 2007-2008 made clear there is the need to readdress and redesign business models and re-balance corporate power in order to broaden the dialogue on responsible investment.

Taking into account this background, Part III outlines the current challenges of the private equity industry under the "new normal": disruptive innovations, regulatory and tax reform, high values of deals and high competition, among others. These ideas shed light on the understanding of the complex ethical challenges at stake, considering the tensions between short-term profits, regulatory targets, free market equilibria, and responsible investment.

In short, the book aims to prepare the reader for participating in a fruitful debate. The main target is the transformation of the global economy to a more just and sustainable one.

PART I: NEW BUSINESS MODELS AND ETHICAL CHALLENGES

Chapter 1

FINANCIALISATION AND THE PRIVATE EQUITY EXPANSION

1.1. CONTEMPORARY GLOBAL CAPITALISM

Since the 1980s, at the heart of the political, economic and social reorganization there has been the search for the re-establishment of the conditions for capital accumulation (Harvey 2007). In this attempt, the growth of the influence of finance over the rest of the economy was best described as the financialisation of capital (Foster 2006) Consequently, there has been noticed a tendency to slow down the accumulation process of real production (Stockhammer 2004).

The 2008 global financial crisis has restated the menace of deep depressions among the current economic challenges while the livelihoods turned out to be subordinated to the bailout of domestic financial systems. Indeed, ten years ago, the collapse of the investment bank Bear Stearns marked a prelude of the financial turmoil. Founded in 1923, it became one of the world's largest investment banks and leader of hedge funds, derivatives and securitization. In January 2008, Moody's downgraded Bear Stearns' mortgage-backed securities and this event put pressure on the bank's liquidity management. After the Federal Reserve interventions to avoid the global spread of systemic risks, Chase purchased Bear Stearns (Amadeo 2018).

The consequences of the 2008 global financial crisis involved the socio-economic structures at worldwide level. Although the crisis was triggered in the financial sector, it marked the culmination of a long-term trend of financialisation of the economic system. After the 1970s, most governments around the world supported the long-run process of neo-liberal reforms that turned out to be characterised by the financialisation of the capitalist economy. In this historical scenario, monopoly-finance capital became increasingly dependent on bubbles that, both in credit and capital markets, proved to be globally the sources of endogenous financial fragility. This process was reinforced, in a vicious circle, by a distribution of income, wealth and power. By negatively influencing labour and working conditions, it rendered increasingly difficult for effective demand to reach (or even approach) the level of full employment. In response to this situation, banking and credit policies also supported by governments and supranational institutions induced consumers to expand their spending.

While public spending on social and infrastructural objectives was severely restricted, it expanded for sustaining the income and the demand of powerful groups. In this situation, corporate decision making was increasingly subordinated to financial commitments. A financial conception of investment gained ground in the context where financial innovations aimed to achieve short-term profits with lower capital requirements. Managers and owners of firms privileged financial gains mostly based on shifts to shareholder values. Changes in corporate ownership, through waves of mergers and acquisitions, created new business models where companies, while highly powerful and concentrated, turned out to be simply bundles of financial assets and liabilities to be traded. Hence, current corporate governance came to have the privilege of mobility, liquidity and short-term profits based on high levels of debt.

Indeed, in contemporary capitalist societies, the current global financial architecture favours the expansion of financial assets, capital mobility and short-term investment decisions – increasingly subordinated to rules of portfolio risk management. In this scenario, changes in production were based on competitiveness and corporate governance criteria. Therefore, job instability and fragile conditions of social protection turned out to put pressure on the redefinition of survival strategies. As a result of the new trends in capital accumulation and production, workers turned out to redefine their skills, become informal entrepreneurs or migrate, among other examples of the current worldwide challenges to citizens. Considering this background, governments faced increasing challenges to support an ethically defensible approach to working conditions. While money is an end in itself social behaviours have mainly turned out to be guided by the profit motive. Consequently, social cohesion was reduced. Indeed, the outstanding conflicts between solidarity and particular interests revealed growing tensions between ethical values and individual principles in capitalist societies.

In his analysis of globalization, Eric Hobsbawm (2007) highlights its extraordinary acceleration since the 1970s that has been characterized by some relevant features. First, contemporary free-markets have ultimately led to an increase in economic and social inequalities not only within states, but also internationally, despite the presence of a decreasing trend in extreme poverty. Second, the self-regulated market has undermined the ability of nation states and welfare systems to protect those who rely on income from wages or salaries. Third, taking into account the social features of globalisation, recent evidence indicates threats to social cohesion and justice in current capitalist societies. Finally, the deep cultural impacts have been strengthened by the diffusion of common values and behaviours privileged by local elites.

Besides these social and economic challenges, the collapse of the international balance of political power since the Second World War has fostered new trends. The political, economic and social dimensions of the recent transformations represent a rupture in relation to the relative order of the Cold War era. From a national perspective, the redefinition and reorientation of the scope of the state actions have re-shaped the relations between the state and corporations. The social and economic impacts of the global governance rules under the Washington Consensus need to be viewed in the context of the global capital accumulation dynamics where the process of investment is increasingly becoming transnational. Nevertheless, the international dimension of investment is overwhelmed by tensions. The transnational corporation is nation-based but its reproduction is part of the reproduction of capital at the systemic (international) level. The challenges of growth and development at the beginning of this century are turning out to be more complex and reveal that the world increasingly seems to require supranational solutions to supranational or transnational problems.

Looking back, in the post-war boom era of 1945 to 1971, the US surplus was at the center of the global economic order. Throughout the Bretton Woods period, the United States recycled part of its surplus via foreign direct investment – mainly in Western Europe and also in Japan. Within the system of international economic flows, the US exported goods to the rest of the world and also finance these purchases. Besides, the US created demand for the exports of foreign countries, primarily Germany and Japan. After the 1970s, this system of international economic flows changed. From 1971 to 2008, the international economic system built after the 1970s was called the "Global Minotaur" by Yanis Varoufakis (2013). According to him, the whole world surpluses aimed to finance the unsustainable expansion of a double deficit: the American trade surplus turned into a large and increasing deficit that joined the government deficit to form the twin deficits. These twin deficits characterize the "Global Minotaur era".

Without Wall Street institutional set up recycling the global surpluses, the US had not been able to hold its twin deficits. Indeed, the new global order after the 1970s was supported thanks to the close collaboration of the expansion of high finance overwhelmed by the political power of economic neo-liberalism. Besides, the global expansion of corporations and supply chains enhanced business models based on increasingly lower wages. The global surplus recycling mechanism reversed the flow of global trade and capital flows. The United States provided sufficient demand for manufacturing in foreign countries – mainly China – in return to capital inflows. As a matter of fact, between 1971 and 2008, the era of high finance supported the expansion of global trade at the cost of financial bubbles, corporate mega-profits and increasing social inequalities. In this scenario, mainstream economics supported the free market efficiency discourse.

However, accordingly Varoufakis (2013), the "Global Minotaur" has a crucial weakness. Indeed, the last cause of the 2008 financial turmoil has been the Minotaur's dynamics that is synonymous to the current global asymmetries. Indeed, the American supremacy requires global permanent unbalances. Consequently, the current global surplus recycling mechanism could not stabilize the world economy. Besides, the mobility of capital flows does not promote the stability of the global financial markets despite prudential measures and supervision practices. Indeed, no global authority is able to make political decisions to overcome these challenges (Hobsbawm 2007). Indeed, power, finance and global governance are related issues that shape livelihoods. In truth, since the beginning of the 20th century the dollar diplomacy has been proposing not only a set of recommendations for global economic integration, but has also enhanced a process of homogenization of attitudes and behaviours all round the world (Rosenberg 1982).

Therefore, we believe that the access to international finance interacts with cultural features in business and society.[1] Modern Western societies and culture have been configured by big business and managers. In the last five decades, diverse growth models have overwhelmed the global scenario: while some countries have presented a consumption-driven growth model fueled by credit, generally followed by current account deficits, other countries have developed an export-driven growth model, mainly characterized by high surpluses in current accounts and low consumption growth. Despite specific growth patterns, the finance-led accumulation regime has presented some distinctive features in labour markets.

In this scenario, how companies operate and what kind of strategic planning dominates have been intimately linked to the continuous growth of private equity (PE) funds – also called the new drivers of globalisation in a complex new set of interrelated balance sheets and cash flows between the income-producing and the financial systems (ITUC 2007). Although substantial heterogeneity exits across the private equity industry one of the

---

[1] Thorstein Veblen, for instance, in his 1899 book *The Theory of the Leisure Class*, wrote a deep analysis of the economic and social implications of the transformations in corporate management and the dominance of finance in modern capitalism that turned out to enhance mergers, acquisitions and minority investors' concerns.

main strategies of PE funds has been characterized by leverage buyouts (Kaplan e Schoar 2003).

Looking back, the first true private equity fund can probably be credited to have been KKR, which was formed in 1976 and raised its first institutional fund in 1978 following the revision of the Employee Retirement Income Security Act which paved the way for greater investments into these types of financial vehicles. In this year, KKR completed the largest take-private of all time with the acquisition of the publicly traded Houdaille Industries for US$380 million.

The PE industry is anchored on the productive sector but aims liquidity. Since the late 1970s, the industry's growth followed a boom/bust cycle pattern. Throughout the first cycle, during the 1980s, the expansion of many of the buyouts was nurtured by junk bonds (also known as High Yield bonds). For instance, the acquisition of RJR Nabisco took place - a private equity deal that was well described by Bryan Burrough and John Helyar in the 1989 book *Barbarians at the Gate: The Fall of RJR Nabisco*.

The collapse of the junk bond market, the first boom/bust cycle ended. After the mid-1990s, many PE leveraged buyouts revealed the recovery of the PE industry, such as Duane Reade (1997), J. Crew (1997), Domino's Pizza (1998), and Petco (2000). However, on behalf of the burst of the tech bubble and the Dotcom crash, many private equity funds, mainly in the telecommunications sector, were hardly hit from the crash while the lack of liquidity in the high-yield bond markets made difficult the buyout activity. In the early 2000s, the private equity deals entered a new period of high growth and mega-buyouts fueled by i) a low interest rate scenario that enhanced higher endebtedness and ii) increasing regulation of public companies. As a result, the PE industry entered a period of mega-buyouts and the industry witnessed strong growth around the world, including in the European and Asian regions.

Regarding this scenario, one of the contemporary challenges that the PE industry faces is the challenge of overcoming "short-termism" in business. Beyond short-termism, the underlying investment pattern expresses new institutional arrangements between financial and productive investment flows. In the last decades, private equity funds' buyouts have not only nurtured the credit market and the corporate bonds' expansion but also defined new parameters to corporate management and profitability. According to Samuelson (2007), after the 1990s, PE buyout companies got and average annual returns higher than the Standard & Poor's 500 index. However, the private equity investors who sit on the board of directors always face conflicting duties. These challenges have been fully described by Hill and Gambaccini (2003, 37): " As a private equity investor, he owes a duty to his fund and its investors to maximize their return. However, as a director of the portfolio company, he owes a duty to act in the best interests of the company."

Indeed, tensions between private money, business practices and welfare have emerged. Indeed, the outstanding contemporary economic challenges related to PE funds should be analyzed in a broader context and in a broader and longer perspective.

1.2. PRIVATE EQUITY AS DRIVERS OF FINANCIALISATION

Global PE assets under management valued at US$2.83tn in June 2017 (Preqin 2018b). The financial practices are, in truth, mechanisms that promote the expansion of global financial markets and influence wealth transfers and labour relations. In fact, PE funds have been key actors in the financialisation of the global economy with deep effects on labour challenges (Jacoby 2008). Lying at the juncture of the real economy and the financial economy, private equity funds draw upon capital and debt in the financial markets to acquire stakes in companies that are intended to be sold for profit after a number of years. The new investment and portfolio management practices have reinforced "short-termism" in American and European business scenario. Indeed, "Short-termism is institutionalized at the workplace and in society" (IUF 2008, 24). At this respect, it is also worth remembering that Kevin Phillips warned that the loosening monetary and credit policies turned out to benefit the minority finance and banking sector, since "finance distributes its concentrated profits to a much smaller slice of the population" (Phillips 2006, 281).[2] As a matter of fact, the PE business model has grown in relevance in the context where financial innovations aimed to achieve fast growth with lower capital requirements could be used by managers to favor short-term financial performance (Fligstein 2001).

Taking into account that financialisation enhances the redistribution and reallocation of power and wealth, Lavoie (2004), Pilkington (2009), Seccareccia (2012) and Passarella (2014) analysed changes in the financial-real sector side relationships in the era of financialisation. All these contributions note that financialisation also consists in changes in the surplus and deficit financial positions traditionally attached to household and non-financial business. Commercial banks have expanded money creation and financed households who have increasingly run into deficit positions. Besides, non-financial corporations have been deploying net savings in financial markets in equity buy backs or supporting structured financial assets than using them to support real-side investment. This book takes inspiration for the above literature and casts light on the fundamental links between finance and labour in today's monetary economy of production. It is not possible to deepen our understanding on the PE business model without the relations among money, output, production, investment and income (Rochon and Rossi 2013, 211).

PE funds became "the most voracious acquirers of assets globally" (Dixon 2007, C12). The typical funds are venture capital, leveraged buyout and mezzanine. In the period between 1998 and 2003, their expansion was focused on leveraged buyout deals and in the aftermath of the early 2000s internet bubble, there was a reduction of venture capital deals (Probitas Partners 2004).

PE funds have assumed a key role in the diversification of investments, based on expectations of high returns and liquidity. Mainly after 2002, the new PE cycle was nurtured by the US expansionary monetary policy and loose lending standards, besides the new regulation standards for public

---

[2] Like Great Britain in the 19th, the United States shifted from manufacturing and the production of goods and services to finance and speculation, *"as the imperial apogees approached, the potential return from investing money domestically came to seem inadequate, and . . . creditors and financial classes began to move more and more funds into overseas investments"* (Phillips 2006, 306).

companies (Sarbanes Oxley legislation).[3] Among other features, the PE business model became popular because it provides a way for investors to have control over a company's strategy, management, and financial decisions—without the disclosure requirements and regulatory oversight faced by publicly traded firms.

As of 2006, private equity funds in the US fundraised more capital than the amount raised in the year of 2000 (Taub 2007). Since then, in Europe, the scale and diversification of these funds now fully match the American ones (Tannon and Johnson 2005). Among larger companies, private equity investment was responsible for a great number of mergers and acquisitions—processes that are usually disruptive to workers. Although US private equity firms are dominant, PE firms have moved towards Europe, Asia and Latin America. In China, they have grown from only 10 in 1995 to more than 6,000 in recent years.

Table 1. Private equity firms: Number of firms and assets under management, 2000-2016, selected years, in US$billion

Year	Number of PE firms	Assets under management
2000	577	1,608
2002	593	2,077
2007	1,468	3,345
2008	1,421	3,584
2009	1,575	3,742
2012	1,940	4,093
2014	2,239	4,443
2016	2,486	4,779

Source: Preqin apud Heberlein (2018). https://www.toptal.com/finance/private-equity-consultants/private-equity-industry.

Note: PE funds are specialized in buyout, the secondary market, funds of funds, besides growth and venture capital.

---

[3] The United States law Sarbanes–Oxley Act of 2002, known as Sarbanes–Oxley, Sarbox or SOX, has been considered a reaction to corporate bad practices and frauds, such as those that involved Enron and WorldCom. http://frwebgate.access.gpo.gov/cgi-bin/getdoc.cgi? Dbname=107_cong_bills&docid=f:h3763enr.tst.pdf.

During the deal peak of 2006-2007, PE funds expanded their share in the global M&A market to 25%. Consequently, the American private equity business model became globalized and European countries, for instance, started to follow its practices (Robertson 2015). In this setting, the financialisation of management practices has been associated to the role of PE managers in the selection of investments of high profit potential and in leveraged buyouts. These practices nurtured a broader process of financialisation of corporate behaviour while private equity funds emerged as major transnational employers.

PRIVATE EQUITY INDUSTRY: HIGHLIGHTS

- The North American private equity market is by far the largest in terms of value and in terms of number of people employed. The second most relevant world region in terms of value of deals is Europe, with China increasingly becoming a big market.
- Historically, most of buyout deals have been focused on consumer goods and financial industries.
- Between the years 2000 and 2016, the number of PE firms globally has tripled and the amount of assets under management (AUM) has grown from almost US$600 billion in 2000 to almost US$2,500 billion.
- Nowadays, the PE industry is entering a "maturity phase" with high competition and higher valuations. This scenario has been challenging the funds´ managers (General Partners) to find attractive deals and to get short-term profits.
- Today, the PE industry is facing increased regulatory pressure, besides investor scrutiny as many limited partners have started to demand a more favourable fee structure.
- PE funds have been committed to innovation regarding technology, efficiency in operating models, portfolio management and new strategic synergies in their investments.

Source: Heberlein (2018).

Soon after the financial global crisis, large private equity deals have revealed the growing difficulties to manage cash flows because of the credit squeeze. Ten years after the global crisis, however, the quantitative easing policy promoted the expansion of the PE industry. According to the Bain & Company (2018a) report on this industry, in the overall, the year of 2017 was a year of increasing investment, strong exit markets, attractive returns and hot fund-raising activity. Table 1 shows the growth of the number of PE firms and the volume of assets under management. Despite private equity funds buy and sell companies in virtually every industry, Jacoby (2008) argued that in spite of the enormous literature on financial development and inequality, few studies consider the intersection between financial markets and the labour markets.

1.3. WHY PRIVATE EQUITY BUSINESS MATTERS TODAY

Before the 2008 global financial crisis, PE investment flows were subordinated to the evolution of financial engineering and rationalization strategies. IUF report (2008b) presents outstanding examples. In 2005 the Danish telecommunications operator TDC was taken over by a group of five of the biggest PE firms - Permira, Apax, Blackstone Group, KKR and Providence Equity for €12 billion. Over 80% of the purchase price was debt financed and the company's debt to asset ratio jumped from 18% to over 90%. Soon after, almost half the company's assets were distributed in shares to the new owners and managers. After some years, TDC was no longer a leader in wireless technology because it radically reduced the investment levels. In the food sector, Findus, Nestlé's frozen foods division with 14 plants and 3,400 employees in Europe, was acquired by the Swedish private equity fund EQT in 2000. At the time of the acquisition, Findus had 14 plants in Europe with 3,400 employees. In 2006, there were 6 plants with 2,900 workers and the company was sold to another financial investor.

After the 2008 financial crisis, more fund managers started to search for good deals that rose steadily each year and amounted 7,775 in 2017. Ten years after the crisis, the expansion of megafunds - those with more than US\$5 billion in assets – has been a reaction to the uncertain market scenario. According to the Bain & Company (2018a) report, the US\$24.7 billion Apollo Investment Fund IX was the largest single buyout fund raised in history and KKR's \$9.3 billion Asian Fund III was the largest-ever buyout fund in Asia.

The Bain report also highlights that, as of 2017, the level of value of public-private deals was still bellow compared with those that preceded the global financial crisis. Indeed, though the global value of buyouts grew 19% from 2016 to 2017, to US\$440 billion, the number of global deals grew 2%, to 3,077 deals. This result shows a reduction of 19% when compared the total value of buyout deals as of 2017 in comparison to 2014 that was the record mark for deal activity in the current economic cycle. While PE investors are aware of the market overheating, some megadeals occurred in 2018 such as JAB Holding Company's US\$7.5 billion buyout of Panera Bread and Sycamore's US\$6.8 billion Staples buyout.

In the PE industry, high competition for assets and record-high value of deals are signals of the increasingly difficult to find new targets and close transactions at attractive prices. In this context, the so called "add-ons" investments have grown in relevance and amounted nearly 50% of the total deals. This new trend can be explained because i) add-ons tend to be smaller deals than the platform ones; ii) the investments in add–ons require less capital.

Today, the disconnection between the total value and the number of deals reflects the current world financial challenges. Although there is enough global liquidity, there are few attractive company targets on which to invest it. Indeed, the monetary policy centered on quantitative easing has been a driver of PE deals and fueled asset prices. In this setting, average purchase price in leveraged buyouts (LBOs) rose to historic high levels but a higher ratio of equity to debt decreases the deal's internal rate of return (IRR). As a result, there is an increasing competition between corporate buyers and PE managers in the middle market, mainly among those funds specialize in the acquisition of smaller companies. According to Bain & Company (2018a), corporate buyers have been active buyers in the middle market and they focus on product development, distribution networks and new brands. For instance, Conagra acquired Thanasi Foods and Angie's Artisan Treats; Nestlé buyout Blue Bottle Coffee.

Regarding the venture capital deals, tech players like Google, Intel and Dell still account for relevant VC deals, as well as companies like Unilever and Kellogg. Besides, the number of investors, and the average deal size have grown steadily.

Despite the relevance of private equity funds, the average citizen might not directly realized the ways in which the PE business model is having an impact upon corporate strategy and governance. This book aims to fill the gap in the existing literature and foster a greater understanding of the current social and economic challenges. Nowadays, the main questions at stake are:

- How can private equity funds generate the attractive returns their limited partners expect in the current scenario of high competition?
- Whether private equity funds may favour employability and decent working conditions while guaranteeing the expected returns to investors?
- Why does the private equity business matter today to rebalance the global economy?

And, above all, which private equity governance could enhance the reconciliation between ethics and new business models?

1.4. GLOSSARY

Add-on Acquisition: It is the acquisition where a private equity (PE) portfolio company acquires another company to enhance growth through product lines or plants.

Alternative Assets: These assets refer to derivatives, hedge funds, private equity, and real estate investments, among others.

Buyout: This is a transaction where a PE fund acquires control of a company.

Called Capital: This is the total aggregate investment that a PE fund has called from investors.

Carried Interest: It is one type of the total fees obtained by GPs.

Carve-Out: This kind of transaction refers to the acquisition of a company by a PE fund- often a publicly-traded company.

Co-investment: It happens when Limited Partners invest directly into a fund's portfolio company.

Crowdfunding: Lower amounts of money and high number of investors are part of the fundraising process.

Dividend recapitalization: This strategy refers to financial restructuring when the company debt is refinanced and aims to pay special dividends.

Dry powder: Amount of uncalled capital within the balance-sheets of PE funds. Also called Capital Overhang.

Early-stage: It refers to the strategic stage of financing focused on venture capital funds that aim developing initial technology/products/services in their portfolio companies.

EBITDA- Earnings before Interest Taxes and Amortization: Financial indicator that measures performance and it is used in the valuation of PE deals.

Exit: This transaction is related to divestment strategies.

Family Office: It refers to the entity created by wealthy families to manage their assets and investments.

Fund-of-Funds: It is an investment vehicle created to invest in a portfolio of funds.

General Partner (GP): It is an entity that manages the fund.

Institutional Investor: This investor centralizes money and makes investments, such as sovereign wealth funds, pension funds, insurance companies, foundations and endowments.

Internal Rate of Return (IRR): It is the annualized rate of return.

Limited Partner (LP): It refers to investors in the PE funds.

Management Fee: It is charged by the General Partners to rung the daily operation of the fund.

Mezzanine Financing: It is a form of debt financing used in leveraged buyouts that is subordinated to a bank debt, but senior to all equity.

Middle Market: It refers to the share of the PE industry where the target companies are middle market companies.

Portfolio Company: It is a company in which a PE equity fund has invested.

Recapitalization: It is a capital restructuring between equity and debt.

Secondary/Secondaries: It is a transaction where a PE portfolio company is sold to another investor in a private sale.

Transaction Fees: These fees are charged to the portfolio companies and they are related to the initial investment or to future acquisitions.

Venture Capital: A PE venture capital (VC) is a private equity fund that specializes in early-stage or startup companies. VC funds typically have a higher tolerance to risk than other PE vehicles.

Chapter 2

THE PRIVATE EQUITY BUSINESS MODEL

2.1. OLD AND NEW BUSINESS MODELS

The 2008 global financial crisis has restated the menace of deep depressions among the current challenges while the livelihoods turned out to be subordinated to the bailout of the financial systems. Looking backward, in the context of the 1930 Great Depression, John Maynard Keynes (1936) called attention to the fact that the capitalist system has endogenous mechanisms capable of destabilizing the levels of spending, income and employment. Indeed, as Keynes warned, the interactions between business decisions and business growth are particularly influenced by the dynamics of contemporary finance - mostly based upon conventions whose precariousness could dampen the the level of investment. In his view, the expansion of capital markets reinforces the potential conflicts between short-run and long-run strategies and put pressure on business stability.

Business strategies related to long-run investment and profits have varied over time. In the last decades, the financialisation of business has impacted the dynamics and outcomes of value creation across economies and societies. Today, PE funds as a financial phenomenon express the power of centralized money to define not only investment flows but also the models of value creation in business. As these funds have been responsible for a great number of mergers & acquisitions, a broad set of investments and employment standards of millions of workers worldwide. However, their social and economic roles in value creation are controversial.

Looking back, in the context of the post Second World War it was widely spread that for a firm's long-term sustainability and profitability it was necessary to invest in long-term expansion and to improve workers' relative wages. Hobsbawm (1995) referred to this period as a "golden age" arguing that in many countries the patterns of living improved. This was also a "golden age" for workers' rights and organization practices. The researchers Lazonick and O'Sullivan (2000) have described this business trend as a strategy of 'retain and reinvest' where profits were retained by the company and reinvested into productive capacity.

However, this scenario began to change during the 1970s and 1980s. The new phase of financial dominance was concomitant with the reconfiguration of the international monetary system under the dollar supremacy after the 1980s that fostered the processes of globalisation and financial deregulation (Madi 2014). As a result, the historical changes in business have been related to qualitative transformations in capital accumulation and competition.

The changing practices of corporate finance fostered the growth of the participation of institutional investors, such as pension funds or private equity firms, in business management as relevant shareholders. As a result, there was a change from reinvestment towards a strategy of maximizing short-term value for shareholders. The drive to increase the share-holders' value and the incorporation of the managerial strata through share options tended to postpone long-term investments. In addition, these practices stimulated mergers & acquisitions and fostered financial speculation. As a matter of fact, the financial conception of investment increased in the context where financial innovations aimed to achieve fast growth with lower capital requirements could be used by managers to adopt a short-term financial performance (Fligstein 2001).

In fact, the process of capital centralization, through waves of mergers and acquisitions, created new challenges to business stability. In this scenario, the economic and social outcomes have involved a trend to 'downsize and distribute', that is to say, a trend to restructure, reduce costs and focus on short-term gains. In practice this has meant plants displacement and closures, changing employment and labour conditions, outsourcing jobs, besides the pressure on supply chain producers in the global markets. The costs fall disproportionately on labour because the new priorities of shareholders limit the social responsibility of firms. As recalled by Froud et al. (2000) "labour is usually the first casualty of restructuring at company level."

There is no doubt that since 1970s the processes of financial deregulation and financialisation have radically changed the way banks, non-banks and non-financial institutions work and interact with the real economy. Within this setting, the dimension and composition of the balance sheets of the different sectors of the economy have changed. Among the main transformations: i) commercial banks, although they still perform their function of creating new purchasing power *ex-nihilo* and continue to provide initial finance to both non-financial business and households, they have been ensuing major increase in cash assets, ii) the household sector has got increasingly indebted, iii) corporations have moved to "surplus units" running financial surpluses that have been diverted towards the acquisition of financial assets instead of financing physical investments, iv) the balance sheets of shadow banking institutions are now larger that before the crisis and influence the investment flows in companies. In short, the financial markets have not only grown in size but also change their composition: the changing role of traditional banks and the expansion of the shadow banking system have become the main features of current financialisation. The dilution of the traditional distinction between bank-centered and market-centered institutional set ups imposed by the post-World War II tight regulation of the financial system has created new analytical challenges.

Accordingly the OECD database, a complex investment chain has enhanced the concentration of wealth and power (Çelik and Isaksson 2013). Regarding the evolution of the business models since the 1990s, the corporations' strategies turned out to focus on short-term gains and the distribution of dividends to shareholders, that is to say, to investors (Lazonick and O'Sullivan 2000). In other words, the business model of large enterprises may be apprehended as a form of governance that aims at increasing short-term earnings by means of a "clash of rationalization". In this context, managers have stimulated the re-composition of tasks, labour turnover, the dismissal of workers and outsourcing (IUF 2007). Therefore, competitiveness and productivity have been put together in the attempt to promote higher business performance. Not only operational strategies in production (suppliers, labour, etc.) but also marketing and commercialisation strategies (logistics, mark-up, market share, customer relationship, etc.) have been relevant to face the productivity challenges and efficiency targets.

In this scenario, new rules of corporate governance aim to overcome "asymmetric information" and offer greater transparency to investors (Fligstein 2001). These governance rules could reduce asymmetric information in capital markets and spread out practices to minimize conflicts between investors and managers.

Private equity funds belong to a complex landscape of institutional investors that could be bifurcated as traditional (i.e., pension funds, investment funds including mutual funds, and insurance companies) and alternative (i.e., sovereign wealth funds, private equity, hedge funds). In the PE business model, Limited Partners (LPs) invest money into the private equity fund where General Partners (GPs) are responsible for managing the fund assets. The GPs define the targets to invest and affect the strategies at the company level.

Among the PE strategies, the expectations about the exit conditions become crucial because of the search for liquidity. Although these institutions hold illiquid assets (companies), managers are used to continuously re-evaluate the portfolio assets. On behalf of his concern on the stability of economic growth, Keynes deepened his understanding of the behaviour of different social groups. In *The General Theory*, Keynes (1936) highlighted the outcomes of modern financial markets and practices. In this setting, he established differences between old and new business models. This historical approach shows that, in the old business model, there was an irrevocable commitment towards investment. Taking into account the new business model, the decisions about what amount and where to invest in the long-run are no more an irrevocable commitment for investors. Indeed, in the new business models, long-term investments are not irrevocable because of the overwhelming liquidity targets.

Within the PE institutional set up, investors and managers do not have an irrevocable commitment to a long-term investment scenario. In the last decades, the burgeoning emphasis on short-term performance, and the new role of portfolio managers had a profound impact on investment strategies, most obviously in soaring portfolio turnover. Short-term decisions became business as usual while daily asset revaluations became benchmark to future investments. Though capital markets might primarily facilitate wealth transfers, daily revaluations impact the path of future investments.

In the context of exit strategies, investments that are fixed for society turn out to be liquid for investors. Today, the dominance of a culture based on liquidity and short-term returns has major social implications. As Keynes warned "Of the maxims of orthodox finance none, surely, is more anti-social than the fetish of liquidity, the doctrine that it is a positive virtue on the part of investment institutions to concentrate their resources upon the holding of 'liquid' securities" (Keynes 1936, 12 V). Indeed, this maxim forgets that there is no such thing as liquid investment for the community as a whole. The increasing search for "liquidity" is incompatible with the society claims for job creation and income growth. When investors demand short-term results and companies respond accordingly, there is a heavy pressure to: a) reduce future investments and expenditures on research and development, b) undertake mergers and acquisitions at, sometimes, higher costs and c) reduce workforce costs in order to achieve the short-term profit targets. Therefore, the susceptibility of workers to market conditions is not independent of the global financial structure, nurtured by financial engineering strategies (Gonçalves and Madi 2011).

As a matter of fact, the business scenario can change and new elements might affect investment decisions and value creation. After the 1970s, the reorganization of the markets at the global level has been overwhelmed by the financial logic of investment in a setting characterized by expansion of credit, capital markets' operations and institutional investors (Crotty 2002). Within this framework, the corporations' strategies turn out to focus on short-term gains and the distribution of dividends to shareholders, that is to say, to investors (Lazonick and Sullivan 2000). As Hyman Minsky (1986) claimed, in contemporary capitalism, finance determines the pace of investment since the investment pattern of corporations has been subordinated to financial commitments.

Private equity funds are, in truth, financial actors that promote the predominance of speculation over their companies on behalf of financial engineering. Private equity managers have been spreading, in truth, a business model where the target is to create short-term value in order to sell the portfolio companies years later in a process called divestment (Wheatley 2010). It is worth remembering Keynes's social concern about the role of speculation over companies "(...) speculators may do no harm as bubbles on a steady stream of enterprise. But the position is serious when enterprise becomes the bubble on a whirlpool of speculation. When the capital development of a country becomes a by-product of the activities of a casino, the job is likely to be ill-done" (Keynes 1936, 12 VI).

Indeed, the deep social consequences of the PE business model are relevant for workers and citizens. The clear cut between investors and managers shapes the redefinition of the labour relations and potential economic growth. Taking into account this background, the cutting question related to value creation in the private equity business model is, as Hyman Minsky (1986) warned: "*Who will benefit?*"

2.2. THE MODERN PRIVATE EQUITY BUSINESS MODEL

Michael Jensen (1989), who has been considered the father of the modern private business model, encouraged its emergence to face the longstanding agency problems related to control and use of corporate resources. Within the PE business model, Jensen addressed that investors designate agents to manage the portfolio companies with more effective results than public companies. First, investors may directly put pressure on underperforming managers so as to achieve the targeted goals. Second, those investors directly involved in the business may give strategic orientation for higher returns.[1]

Since PE funds are a financial phenomenon, a company acquisition is equivalent to an addition to a stock of financial assets (Cullen and James 2007). GPs use a combination of equity and debt to access pension funds, insurance companies and endowments to invest in companies that are not traded publicly. Table 2 shows that the features of private equity funds can vary substantially across the global industry. At the core of the business model, most companies are privately held. One of the most relevant types of private equity business is the buyout fund. In this case, the PE fund gains majority control of a portfolio company through the use of debt. This financial strategy can be risky if the acquired firm's cash flow is uneven and the company's ability to service its debt is low. Analysing the risk profile, Weidig and Mathonet (2004) addressed that in venture capital deals the probability of a total loss of the capital invested is around 30%. However, in PE buyouts, the risk happens to be much lower (Metrick and Yasuda 2007).

Table 2. Private equity funds by type: Main features

Private Equity by type	Main features
Leveraged Buyout (LBO)	PE funds acquire control of an operating company with debt.
Venture Capital (VC)	PE funds invest in early-stage companies with significant growth prospects
Growth	PE funds invest in already existing companies.
Secondaries	This transaction refers to a PE portfolio company being sold to another a private sale before the target holding period.
Fund of Funds	A Fund of Funds invests in portfolio companies of PE funds.

Source: Elaborated by the author. Adapted from Glossary of Private Equity and Venture Capital Terms (2019). http://www.allenlatta.com/glossary-of-private-equityterms.html.

Figure 1 shows the main components of a typical PE business structure. The governance practices in this industry have historically been shaped by

---

[1] Scholes et al. (2009) found out a greater scope for efficiency gains and expansion in cases where the founder is present at the time of the buyout.

the expectations of Limited Partners (investors) and General Partners (managers) that privileged liquidity and high short-run performance incentives. Decisions about the choice of portfolio companies have been influenced by the potential market growth and short-term profits (up to 3-5 years), besides legal and incentive structures, among other factors. After the acquisitions, the cash-flow generation - to pay fees, dividends and debts - require that the General Partners focus on cost reductions and labour relations. Consequently, the reorganization of production usually redefines tasks and the control of workers in a context characterized by turnover, outsourcing and casual work. Nevertheless, the Bain & Company (2018) report highlights that PE buyout funds, mainly after the global crisis, have been adopting strategies beyond high leverage and cost rationalization. One relevant example of the new trend refers to active commercial programs to enhance organic growth. Indeed, private equity managers cannot mainly rely on a financial approach to achieve attractive returns, but they need to know how the markets work (Alvarez and Jenkins 2007, 27).

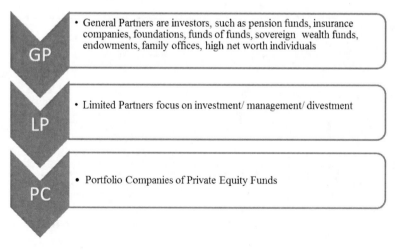

Source: Elaborated by the Author.

Figure 1. Main Components of a Typical Private Equity Business Structure.

Taking into account the PE business dynamics, the conditions of entry in new markets are cyclical: they are generally easy following a boom

(Kaplan and Schoar, 2003). After the acquisitions, the main stages of the private equity business model are:

1. The Limited Partners provide capital to the fund.
2. The General Partners select the portfolio companies.
3. In leveraged buyouts, General Partners increase the amount of debt as part of the financial strategies aimed to reduce the amount of capital called.
4. The General Partners introduce tax planning and operational strategies to reduce costs and increase value creation.
5. The General Partners search for exit strategies after 3-5 years: make IPOs, sell the company to a strategic corporation or to another private equity firm.

2.3. A PRAGMATIST APPROACH TO ETHICS IN BUSINESS MODELS

The main features of the private equity governance open new philosophical perspectives to study, in a Pragmatist approach, the social and institutional challenges related to business models in contemporary globalisation. In line with the Pragmatist contribution of the American philosopher Charles S. Peirce, a deep study of social wealth, highlights the overwhelming role of economic institutions as powerful social institutions that embrace systems of belief. According to Houser (2016a), Peirce attributed minds to institutions and social groups in behalf of his belief that they are "greater persons", that is to say, living communities with collective personalities. In fact, social institutions can be thought as minded institutions that are reservoirs of *social habits*, that is to say, of social beliefs related to cultural practices (customs, language, religion, artworks and artefacts) that support and maintain a civilization. Besides, social minds are relational networks.[2] At this respect, among social psychologists, George Herbert

---

[2] At this respect, among social psychologists, George Herbert Mead believed that social mind has an essential role in the emergence and functioning of individual human minds and the

Mead believed that the social mind has an essential role in the emergence
and functioning of individual human minds. Self-conceptions are the result
of these interactions.

Peirce's contemporary relevance relies on his concern with actual life
(Ibri 2017). Under his philosophical contribution, the function of economic
institutions should be to sustain beliefs, practices and values that are relevant
at a fundamental level of sustainable human livelihoods. In accordance to a
Pragmatist analysis of institutions, the social mind is separated from the
individual human mentality that constitutes its own network of beliefs and
might acquire its own identity. As a result, powerful institutions have
evolved to support these two great classes of human endeavor: i) those of
vital importance concerning the practical needs of life and related to firm
beliefs, and ii) those pertaining to human aspirations, mainly the search for
knowledge and truth, and related to provisional beliefs. Besides family and
speech, considered as basic human institutions, other relevant institutions for
social life can be identified—including agriculture, industry, commerce,
games, the arts, religion, schools, laboratories, libraries, museums,
observatories, the sciences; and government.[3]

Under this institutional approach, social minds and their interrelations
with multiple individual minds foster semiotic systems. Individuals' patterns
of behaviour (including habits and patterns of thought) depend not only on
instinctive behaviours and on direct learning from experience, but also on
the social minds (as cognitive systems) of the institutions they belong to. As
these institutions accumulate specialized knowledge, individuals'
intellectual capacity increase, shape cultures and preserve civilizations. Over
generations, civilizations have been developing different social institutions
throughout a process where those successful habits that emerged from trials
and errors contribute to the preservation and advancement of culture. As a
matter of fact, the Peircean doubt-belief process might be taken into account
in the analysis of social minds. Settled beliefs (behavioural habits) remain

---

development of self-conceptions is a result of these interactions. Houser (2016a) notes that
similarities between Meade and Peirce should be developed in further research. Houser also
points to the potential dialogue between cognitive science and Peirce.
[3] According to Max H. Fisch, apud Houser (2016a).

unchanged up to be disturbed by doubt that result from inadequate institutional responses to conflicts or disturbances. These conflicts either might threaten the survival or well-being of the group or even the achievement of some common purpose. Only satisfactory responsive actions will adapt individual and social minds to changing environmental realities.

Indeed, a Peircean approach to systems of belief is relevant for developing a Pragmatist approach to ethics. This approach privileges the concept of norms as social beliefs related to institutions as cultural practices that emerge in a non-deterministic evolutionary process. Moreover, those norms that support and maintain a civilization result from an ongoing social dialogue that is open to transformation.

Systems of belief can be understood as signs, or triadic relations that are rooted in social principles and involve an evolutionary process of interpretation of the experience that involves intelligibility and meaning. As a semiotic process of thought and representation it is ultimately embedded in the concrete and practical relationships that constitute the world and it is future-oriented. Systems of belief are those aspects of reality that human beings use to interpret, communicate and act. In this perspective, there is a dynamic interplay between norms as signs and collective life. We can say that institutions as systems of belief convey the generality of the habits of behaviour. Since the process of semiosis is interactive and continuous, beliefs may change (Peirce, CP 4.237). Under this approach, beliefs are never aprioristic but result of a process of interpretation that is non-deterministic.

Beliefs, as habits of behavior that refer to cognitive experiences, are regular. In this line of philosophical development, systems of beliefs refer to a generalization of habits within society (Peirce, CP 5.417). According to Peirce, "Habits only come about by reiteration" (Peirce, CP 5.487). However, habits of behaviour endure for some time until individuals meet some challenges in the daily routines that may foster their dissolution. The role of Chance in breaking habits is decisive in an evolutionary perspective of institutions and societies.

The American philosopher has the merit of rejecting the mechanistic and adaptive perspective of evolution where habits show only inertia (Peirce EP

2, 205). In this approach, the reality of Chance - diversity, irregularity and asymmetry that are immediately present in the facts of experience - rejects the doctrine of necessitarianism in social life. Since, new habits may emerge and they may gradually become more generalized, the evolution of systems of belief exhibits a degree of freedom. As a result, this approach to institutions as systems of beliefs presupposes that uncertainty overwhelms social dynamics. This uncertainty is not epistemological, but rather ontological. Let us recall Peirce's words: "Remark, reader, at this point, that Chance, whether it be absolute or not, is not the mere creature of our ignorance. It is that diversity and variety of things and events which law does not prevent. Such is that real Chance upon which the kinetical theory of gases, and the doctrines of political economy, depend" (Peirce, CP 6.612).

Indeed, the presence of Chance as a realistic ontological principle gives rise to discontinuities between the past and the future that add some degree of indeterminacy to the evolution of systems of beliefs within economic, social and political contexts. In this setting, the plasticity of minds to face changing external drivers allows for the development of new beliefs; this plasticity requires "a new observational means" in order to draw attention to new relations between new facts (Peirce, CP 1.109).

What Peirce highlights is that deliberate transformation of habits within institutions requires uberty: first in assessing the changes on the outer world and second in developing new habits (Peirce EP 2, 463). Uberty is a crucial feature of reasoning that presents certain degree of looseness and, therefore, it copes with spontaneous developments.

However, the Peircean view highlights that habit-changing involves a cognitive process. This process is not fully predictable since steady habits many be dominant (Peirce, CP 1.107). Besides the weight of inertia, habit-changing involves new interpretations and, therefore, the possibility of error. Indeed, the Peircean perspective opens up a vision of institutions in evolution where the constraints of reality lead to revising erroneous propositions and producing new interpretations, habits, beliefs and actions through the flow of time.

The American philosopher not only highlighted that a "man is essentially a social animal" (Peirce, CP 1.11), but also that economic institutions embrace systems of beliefs. While analyzing the economic and social challenges of the American liberalism of the nineteenth century, Peirce addressed the overwhelming role of economic institutions as powerful social institutions that embrace norms as systems of belief. His concern about the relationship between institutions and human behaviour is deep, as his writing shows:

> Food for whom? Why, for the greedy master of intelligence. I do not mean to say that this is one of the legitimate conclusions of political economy, the scientific character of which I fully acknowledge. But the study of doctrines, themselves true, will often temporarily encourage generalizations extremely false, as the study of physics has encouraged necessitarianism. What I say, then, is that the great attention paid to economical questions during our century has induced an exaggeration of the beneficial effects of greed and of the unfortunate results of sentiment, until there has resulted a philosophy which comes unwittingly to this, that greed is the great agent in the elevation of the human race and in the evolution of the universe (Peirce, CP 6.290)

It is clear that the author argued against the "popular" socio-economic interpretation of Darwinism of the late nineteenth century since this interpretation hinders social well-being by fixing beliefs in the "beneficial effects of greed". At his time, the philosopher criticizes the utilitarian normative ethics theory where the hedonistic calculus of pleasure and pain serves as universal criteria for human action. Peirce is perfectly clear: "greed" is the economic perversion of a Pragmatist ethics. In his opinion, the nineteenth century that he called the "economical century" has been driven by self-love and the love of a limited class with shared common interests. The relevant issue at stake is that Peirce's concern about the evolution of institutions put in question the relationship between norms, systems of belief and the social well-being.

Under a Pragmatist perspective, reasoning is embedded in social relationships and the direction of its growth involves issues of evaluative order. A relevant implication of the previous reflection, referenced in Peirce's philosophical system, is that although normativity by definition is prescriptive, normativity in the context of the Peircean Pragmatism does not need to prescribe deterministically.

It is worth highlighting that Peirce's Pragmatism refers to a compromise between systems of belief and human conduct that is open to transformation. In this perspective, there is an aesthetic drive of evolution behind a Pragmatist ethical view that enhances the growth in cooperation in social life through time. What is also relevant about the previous reflection on the role of systems of belief and institutions is that the turn to Pragmatism in business should require that business models should be successfully reconciled with meaningful values and ethical ideals.

As a matter of fact, a Pragmatist philosophical approach to ethical business addresses the overwhelming role of economic institutions as powerful social institutions that embrace systems of beliefs. Under a Peircean view, the function of such institutions would be to sustain practices and values that are relevant at a fundamental level of human life. The main question that the philosopher arose is whether those beliefs might foster human life and whether they might be effective in enhancing social cohesion in their cultural communities.

To Peirce, the logical character of the Pragmatist maxim justifies that his approach to social life refuses singular ends. Social ends should be general and social norms depend directly on ethics. At this respect, the *summum bonum* for ethical conduct is the admirable that is situated within the framework of aesthetics.[4]

While aesthetics is fundamental because it considers what it means to be an admirable end, ethics analyzes the ends to which thoughts, beliefs and actions should be directed and logic or semiotics governs thought and aims at truth. Among the normative sciences, Peirce highlights an intimate relationship between ethics and aesthetics. In his words: "But we cannot get any clue to the secret of Ethics . . . until we have first made up our formula for what it is that we are prepared to admire. I do not care what doctrine of ethics be embraced, it will always be so" (Peirce, CP 5.36). Logic, then, is a special case of ethical action, because logic deals with the inferences and

---

[4] Ibri (2002) explains the relations between pragmatism and ethics under a Peircean perspective. The author also highlights that the complexity of the status of ethics in Peirce's thought still remains open to further research.

arguments which we are prepared to approve and, as he wrote later, "such self-approval supposes self-control" (Peirce, CP 5.130).

Contrary to the "Gospel of Greed", a Pragmatist approach to ethical business is rooted in real social needs. Under his evolutionary approach, there is an aesthetic drive of evolution behind an ethical perspective of business. At this respect, Houser (2016a) addresses that natural affinity among humans fosters the formation of social institutions and systems which are generally conducive to beneficial habits and individual well-being. In other terms, this enhances ethic behaviours in social institutions, that is to say, their long-term viability.

In a Pragmatist view, ethical business models require specific habits within institutions since their evolution relies on beliefs that might influence individual and social behaviours. According to this line of thought, the political economy of ethical business models is a social process, not an individual one. As a cultural creation and system of beliefs, economic institutions evolve over time towards ethical concerns when human groups cohere to achieve common purpose(s).

2.4. THE RELEVANCE OF A PRAGMATIST ETHICS

Beyond the expansion of the private equity business model, there is a moral-philosophical consensus about the adoption of an utilitarian framework that highlights the functions performed by self-interest in relation to individual and social welfare. In this setting, a shift to ethical business requires the adoption of new habits in the context of PE governance to cope with current economic and social global challenges.

The recent success of Piketty's book (2014) showed that the interest in this topic has increased. Piketty's 15-year research program focused on the evolution of income and wealth (which he calls capital) in leading high-income countries over the past three centuries. Among the lessons, he outlines the trend to growing economic inequality. While in Europe the so called patrimonial capitalism is being re-created, the "supermanagers" in the US have been main actors in the wealth concentration process.

Among other contributions to re-think the role of investors, managers and the growth in income inequality, Nobel Laureate Joseph Stiglitz's 2012 book, *The Price of Inequality*, argues that there is an interconnection between the pattern of business growth, inequality and wealth. He highlighted the role of credit in wealth expansion, the reduction in the ratio of wages to productivity, the increasing ratio of CEO pay to worker pay and growing market power. In the current business model scenario, weakening workers' bargaining power, increasing capital mobility and abuses of corporate power by CEOs can certainly help to explain the growing levels of income inequality.[5]

We certainly need to reflect on the nexus between the business global scenario and the income and wealth inequality because it encloses the inner tensions between the hypertrophy of finance and the expectations of society about citizenship, labour and income. In this context, the levels of employment have become a key variable in macroeconomic and business adjustments. In contemporary capitalism, global financial architecture enahnced capital mobility and short-term investment – increasingly subordinated to the decisions of "supermanagers" and the rules of portfolio risk management.

Besides, capital mobility enhances growing labour flexibility. While recent changes in productive organization have been based on competitiveness and corporate governance criteria, job instability and fragile conditions of social protection have forced the reorganization of survival strategies. Thus, workers must redefine their skills or become informal entrepreneurs. Given the decreasing power of workers in recent decades, it is not surprising that both the globalisation process and its outcomes foster the concentration of wealth and changes in social behaviour.

Definitely, the governance of PE funds needs to come to terms with wealth concentration and conomic inequality. Concerns with inequality extend well beyond issues of justice and fairness since the outcomes of economic inequality affect not only economic growth and sustainability but also social cohesion and political stability.

---

[5] See also Fullbrook (2011).

PART II: THE PRIVATE EQUITY ECOSYSTEM

In: Private Equity Globalisation   ISBN: 978-1-53615-043-8
Editor: M. Madi   © 2019 Nova Science Publishers, Inc.

Chapter 3

PRIVATE EQUITY FUNDRAISING

3.1. CENTRALIZING MONEY

According to Preqin database, the number of private equity funds closed has been growing since the 2000s (Table 3). PE buyouts were dominant in fundraising in 2016, although the number of Venture Capital (VC) funds was higher in 2016 (Table 4). In the context of quantitative easing polices, the period between 2009 to 2015 has been strong for fundraising, mainly in the mid-market buyout funds (Bain & Company 2015, 7). In the most important market, North-America, fundraising has been led by mega-buyout funds. Looking at the location of PE funds, among the top 100, there is noted a concentration in North America, West Europe and Asia (Table 5).

In fact, according to the Bain & Company (2018a) report, private equity funds have attracted more capital since 2013 than in the five year period that preceded the 2008 global financial crisis. Despite heavy competition in the PE industry, General Partners had been successful in their fundraising efforts. The largest firms, such as KKR, Apollo and CVC also achieved great records of fundraising. As of 2018, the shift to the Asia Pacific area needs to be highlighted. Asia-focused funds grew in number and in aggregate capital raised. Despite European-focused funds experienced a 36% decline in aggregate capital raised in the second quarter of 2018, overall fundraising trends in 2018 remained positive (Preqin 2018a). Concerns over Brexit might have contributed to this result. In this setting, PE firms continue to raise capital for short-term strategies that refer to investments over time periods significantly in excess of the three to five years that are historically typical for the private equity industry.

Table 3. Private equity fundraising: Number of funds closed and aggregate capital raised, 2000-2017, in US$ billion

Year	Number of PE funds closed	Aggregate capital raised
2000	755	207
2003	438	76
2006	934	352
2009	765	213
2012	1,006	234
2015	1,188	344
2016	1,243	414
2017	921	453

Source: Preqin Equity Online.

Table 4. Private equity funds by type: Number and fundraising, 2016, in US$ billion

PE Fund by Type	Number of Funds	Aggregate Capital Raised
Buyout	145	157
Venture Capital	311	48

Source: Preqin apud Heberlein (2018). https://www.toptal.com/finance/private-equity-consultants/private-equity-industry.

Table 5. Private equity fundraising, 2017-2018, in US$ billion

Region	2018(Q2)
North America	36.9
Europe	20.9
Asia	21.9
Rest of the world	5.1

Source: Preqin (2018a). http://docs.preqin.com/quarterly/pe/Preqin-Quarterly-Private Equity-Update-Q2-2018.pdf.

Table 6. Largest private equity funds closed, in proportion of aggregate capital raised, 2015-2017, in %

Year	2015	2016	2017
10 Largest Funds Closed	23	22	28
20 Largest Funds Closed	32	33	42
50 Largest Funds Closed	49	49	59

Source: Preqin Equity Online.

In addition to the shift to the Asia Pacific region, there has been a growth trend in the size of the PE fund (Table 6). Small funds - with less than US$500 million - reduced their participation in fundraising from 36% in 2010 to 20% in 2017. Mid-size funds – with more than US$5 billion-increased their participation in fundraising from 7% in 2010 to 30% in 2017. Despite the scenario dominated by large funds, the smaller ones have continued to grow in recent years.

As a matter of fact, megafunds have grown in the US, Europe and also in Asia where large funds were previously almost nonexistent. As of September 2018, the average size of PE funds increased by 27%, between 2017 and 2018. Buyout funds remain the most active strategy, accounting for 36% of the funds rose, followed by real estate (20%) and infrastructure (13%), according to LPEA (2018a).

3.2. LEVERAGE PRACTICES

In a context of uncertainty, the portfolio management of private equity funds is based on precarious conventions. PE funds are part of a set of interrelated balance sheets and cash flows between the income-producing system (hedge, speculative and Ponzi firms) and the financial structure that affect the valuation of the stock of capital assets, the evolution of credit and the pace of investment. As a matter of fact, the overall results have become highly dependent on financial portfolio management and high leverage. Consequently, the capital accumulation process in the PE industry has been overwhelmed by a "pro-rentier" behavior in the context of financialisation.

Throughout the business cycle, when profits decline, as they inevitably do, credit and external sources of funding generally become restricted and the price of assets also fall. This scenario affects the fundraising of these institutional investors. It is worth noting that the 2008 global credit crisis showed that the use of excessive debt to amplify capital returns reached well beyond the frontiers of private equity leveraged buyouts. However, high leverage turned out to be one of the concerns about the PE industry because of the impacts on operational strategies (Blum 2008).

Loans are an essential component of buyouts because private equity investors typically contribute only with a fraction of the capital needed to complete the deal. Montgomerie (2008) states that PE leveraged buyouts improve returns after loading the acquired companies with debt, up to 70% of the capital structure. In most cases, high leverage in the portfolio companies might privilege short-term returns of the PE funds against their sustainability.

As a result of the 2008 global credit squeeze and the volatility in the valuation of assets in a recessive context, private equity large transactions had difficulties to get the required levels of debt for deals. Besides, the investors' preference for funding large leveraged buyout (LBO) deals deteriorated. Therefore, the volume of LBO deals declined because many of them were withdrawn or postponed. In this scenario of crisis, the default risk of LBO deals increased, particularly for those investments that faced substantial refinancing needs in the short-term since riskier loans with higher borrowing costs rose sharply in a context of moderate corporate cash flows..

Indeed, profitable LBOs require easy access to cheap credit and rising share prices in public equity markets to exit through an IPO. When credit dries up, market disappears for secondary buyouts and it is difficult to refinance existing debts through recapitalization strategies.

After the 2008 turmoil, it was estimated that more than US$500 billion to be refinanced between 2008 and 2010 (BIS 2012). Both the European Central Bank (ECB) and the International Monetary Fund (IMF) expressed concern about the rise in the ratio of leverage. They both mentioned that this level of debt was unsustainable and needed to be seriously monitored. The ECB conjectured that large amounts of debt in companies could have a serious adverse effect on global economic markets. The Bank of England also showed concern about the process of fast and deep corporate re-leveraging.

As a matter of fact, the changes in the way investments are made, in how companies operate and in what kind of strategic planning is dominant in large parts of business is intimately linked to the PE continuous growth - the new economic drivers of globalisation. The expected returns from investments are increasingly determined by financial strategies. Therefore, investments in production, innovation, sales, distribution, and workers are thus subordinated to those strategies. As a result, the planning horizon has become shorter and financial returns are prioritized above real economic performance (ITUC 2007).

Regarding the period before the global crisis, Table 7 shows the relevance of debt for deals.

Table 7. Private equity leverage: Announced us acquisitions, 2005-2007, in %

Private Equity Firm	Leverage Ratio
Madison Dearbon Partners	11.8
Providence Equity Partners	11.0
Blackstone Group	10.6
Thomas H. lee Partners	10.3
Carlyle Group	9.6
Goldman Sachs Group	9.5
Apollo Management	9.1
TPG	8.2
Bain Capital	7.8

Source: Kelly (2007).
Note: Acquisitions that refer to more than US$100 million from January 2005 to September 2007. The leverage ratio is the average amount of debt committed to an acquisition relative to the target's EBITDA.

Indeed, after the 1980s, two significant periods of leveraged buyouts occurred. The first one, confined mostly to North America, happened in the 1980s. The second one, global in scope, began and accelerated at the beginning of the 2000s. Some relevant market features were related to the latest debt cycle:

- Leveraged buyout loans grew much more rapidly than high-yield bonds.
- Banks have been replaced by institutional investors as major sources of funding.
- There was a shift in banking from "buy and hold" to "originate to distribute".
- The emergence of securitization and secondary market trading of leveraged buyout loans enhanced mergers & acquisitions.

Therefore, cyclical and market conditions favoured private equity leveraged deals. In this setting: i) corporate default rates have been low on behalf of the good global macroeconomic backdrop, ii) the risk behaviour of investors enhanced borrower-friendly terms of loan issuance, iii) strong corporate cash flows and low interest rates made takeovers attractive. However, in the mid-2007, the supply of loans became more restrained as the turbulence in financial markets deepened. As a result, global primary market leveraged buyout loan (leverage loan) volumes shrank by more than 50% in the second half of 2007 (BIS 2008). Thus, in late 2007, the current global financial crisis surfaced. When liquidity contracts, exit strategies are revisited and GPs may maintain the portfolio companies for *longer periods* and under even *tighter cash flow constraints* than originally expected.

After mid-2007, banks cancelled some commitments to fund leveraged loans and high-yield bonds in a context of increased funding costs, higher capital requirements and significant mark to market losses (BIS 2008). Investment banks, for instance, temporarily froze lending to fund higher-risk leveraged buyout strategies. In the credit squeeze scenario, private equity funds seek other sources of fundraising such as sovereign wealth funds, which in turn, can minimise their disclosure and transparency by using private equity firms as conduits for buyouts (Blum 2008).

Considering the interconnections between the subprime mortgages and the leveraged loan market in mid-2007, the US federal banking and securities regulators (OCC, the Federal Reserve and SEC) turned out to supervise the commercial and investment banks that financed the recent LBOs since credit market problems raised risk-management concerns. Indeed, JP Morgan Chase, Citibank, Bank of America, Wachovia, Goldman Sachs, Lehman Brothers, Merrill Lynch, and Morgan Stanley were committed to 77% of leveraged loans from 2005 through 2007. Because of the complexity of leveraged transactions and restrictions on commercial bank finance activities, the leveraged financing package was arranged through the bank, its subsidiaries, or its holding company. According to OCC and SEC staff, the major banks generally manage the risk exposures by syndicating their leveraged loans. Before June 2007, the major commercial and investment banks were able to use an "originate-to-distribute" model where a bank or group of banks underwrite a leveraged loan and then syndicate all or some portion of the loan to other institutions. Leading up to June 2007, strong demand of collateralized loan obligations by insurance companies, mutual funds, and hedge funds fostered the growth of the leveraged loan market. However, as of late 2007 and 2008, banks[1] could no longer syndicate some of their leveraged loans at prices they originally anticipated (GAO 2008).

In this credit cycle, loans issued to finance buyouts were typically syndicated—provided by a group of lenders—and categorized as leveraged, rather than investment-grade, loans. Banks and other lenders provided, in total, nearly US$2.7 trillion in syndicated, leveraged loans from 2005 through 2007: of this total 42 % was used to finance LBOs and portfolio companies.

Table 8 shows the largest banks that provided syndicated leveraged loans for private equity buyouts in the US market in the period between 2005 and 2007.

In 2017, liquidity challenges led to a reduction of LBOs deals by private equity funds that put pressure on major banks to hold on their balance sheets more loans than planned- also leveraged loans intended to be syndicated to institutional investors. As a result of the decrease in demand for syndicated

---

[1] In addition to bank loans, PE buyout funds may use high-yield bonds that are debt securities issued by companies with low investment grade ratings.

loans, the banks reduced their earnings after marking down some of their leveraged loans and loan commitments to reflect the lower market prices.

Table 8. Private equity leverage buyouts: Main commercial and investment banks, US market, 2005-2007

Commercial and Investment Banks	Deal Value (US$ billion)	Number of deals	Market share based on value, in %
JP Morgan Chase	95.3	272	15
Goldman Sachs	58.3	129	9.2
Citigroup	56.2	107	8.9
Credit Suisse	54.9	189	8.7
Bank of America	49.6	192	7.8

Source: GAO (2008).

Soon after the crisis, then, the major banks continued to face challenges reducing their loan holdings. First, banks reduced their leveraged finance commitments as liquidity gradually returned to the leveraged finance market, and as some LBO deals have been cancelled, restructured, or repriced. Second, banks continued to reduce their holdings of leveraged loans as they looked for market opportunities to syndicate or sell leveraged loans. Additionally, banks managed their leveraged loan risk exposures through hedging, such as with credit derivatives.

At that time, although the PE leveraged loan market represented a relatively small segment of the financial markets, systemic risk concerns arose. First, the major players included some of the largest US commercial and investment banks. Second, the use of the originate-to-distribute model fostered securitization of leveraged loans. Third, the global turmoil revealed risk-management challenges in banking lending activities. Finally, the originate-to-distribute model transfers risks and reduces transparency about risk concentration. That is why IUF (2007) pointed out that the securitisation of loans do not defer from the traditional subprime mortgages. According to Preqin (2007), the excess liquidity created by private equity was also one of the causes of the 2007 banking liquidity crisis and subsequent recession.

Ten years after the 2008 crisis, the debt markets continue to offer fund transactions with low-cost leverage in both the US and Europe. As a result, the average debt of PE leveraged deals almost amounted 6 times the EBITDA (earnings before interest, taxes, depreciation and amortization), the level at which regulators begin to pay close attention (Bain & Company 2018). For instance, the buyout of USI Insurance Services led by KKR increased the company's leverage ratio just above eight times EBITDA, according to Moody's. This kind of private equity deals has begun to attract higher regulatory scrutiny. Despite the risk concerns, some surveys indicate that for 95% of LPs, returns from private equity have met or exceeded expectations. That kind of outperformance seems to be persistent in a context of low yields on most other investment options (LPEA, 2018). Considering the interconnections between banks and the PE industry, prudential financial regulation presents challenges to the future of PE fundraising and the shadow banking.

Looking back, in the late 1980s, there was a global concern around the development of a new regime of prudential banking regulation, founded on the ratio of capital to risk-adjusted assets. The first Basel Capital Accord introduced the 8% capital requirement on the risk-weighted value of a bank's assets, mainly credit-risk. As of 2004, the Capital Accord Basel II was settled and underlined three pillars: a bank's core capital requirement; supervision and market discipline. This Accord aimed to spread out mechanisms of protection not only to avoid financial systemic risk but also to increase informational transparency (disclosure). Therefore, the institutional set up would enhance more efficient financial leveraged systems and greater transparency to financial regulators and investors.

After the Capital Accord Basel II, banks proved to enhance asset-liability management (ALM), or even, balance sheet management, to reduce legally capital requirements. At the operational level, ALM involves new management practices and techniques to manage risks that arise due to imbalances in assets and liabilities. For example, banks could manage the credit risk with further securitization transactions. ALM could also be used to analyse market risks related to trading in capital markets. Besides, low capital requirements might be supported by off balance sheet assets since great volumes of their trading books could shift into SIVs (structured investment vehicles).

In the aftermath of the 2008 global crisis, the global biggest banks increased write-downs on loans while credit losses put pressure on profitability (BIS 2012). The reduction of the leverage ratio and the new strategies related to the internal reassessment of risks (credit, currency, interest, liquidity) have been implemented to cope with capital requirements. Besides, uncertainty about the future of the global economy has reduced the interest in foreign markets, mainly in Europe and the US. Although Basel II has represented an improvement in terms of prudential banking regulation, the lesson learned is that bank capital requirements are not sufficient to sustain banks' stability. As a matter of fact, in spite of greater risk-sensitivity and comprehensive coverage of the supervision of banking risks, concerns about the weaknesses of the regulatory framework, or even, of the instruments and methods used by regulators have arisen. The global crisis showed that innovations related to asset-liability management have reinforced individual and systemic risks. In this conjuncture, the potential threaten of financial collapse could certainly reduce employment levels and lead to a depression.

In response to the crisis, supervisory authorities have been also shaping firther rules related to Basel III to build a more resilient financial system. Among other issues, i) banks will need to hold larger capital requirements against further potential losses, ii) the approaval of financial products would involve extensive disclosure requirements and iii) banks would be induced to negotiate standardized products (BIS 2012). Besides, the shadow banking institutions – and therefore, the PE funds – have also been the target of part of the set of innovations in regulation.

Despite the lessons from the 2008 financial crisis, Table 9 shows that the role of leverage in private equity investments has been growing since 2004 and, in 2017, the Debt/EBITDA relation almost achieved the 2006 record.

As the repayment of debts put pressure on operational and strategic decisions, high leverage has raised questions regarding its impact on the stability and survival of these companies. However, leverage can also allow private equity firms to get higher total returns. Table 10 outlines the key arguments surrounding the use of leverage and financial engineering in private equity.

Table 9. Private equity investments: Global medium ebitda multiples, 2006-2017, in %

Year	Valuation/EBITDA	Equity/EBITDA	Debt/EBITDA
2006	9.0	3.4	5.6
2008	6.8	3.2	3.6
2009	5.6	2.8	2.8
2010	7.0	3.1	3.9
2012	7.9	3.9	4.0
2014	9.3	4.1	5.2
2016	9.2	4.5	4.7
2017	10.7	5.2	5.5

Source: McKinsey (2018).

Table 10. Private equity leverage and financial engineering: Literature review

Research results	References
Evidences from Germany and the UK show that the generation of cash flows to pay debts has led to a decline in investment for research & development and for capital expenditures.	Montgomerie, J. 2008. "Labour and the Locusts: Private Equity's Impact on the Economy and the Labour Market." *Conference Report of the Seventh British-German Trades Union Forum*, London: Anglo-German Foundation for the Study of Industrial Society.
Before the 2008 financial crisis, the success of PE firms in out bidding publicly-traded wave was related to their source of acquisition financing with debt.	Bartlett, Robert P. 2008. "Taking Finance Seriously: How Debt-Financing Distorts Bidding Outcomes in Corporate Takeovers." *Fordham Law Review*, 76.
PE firms provide their portfolio companies with an increasingly borrowing competitive advantage.	de Fontenay, Elisabeth. 2013. "Private Equity Firms as Gatekeeper." *SSRN*. https://ssrn.com/abstract=2245156
Between 1997 and 2010, the performance of 2,151 PE portfolio companies showed that PE GPs face financial distress relatively efficiently.	Hotchkiss, Edith S., Stromberg, Per and Smith, David Carl. 2014. "Private Equity and the Resolution of Financial Distress." *AFA Chicago Meetings Paper*.

Source: Elaborated by the author. Adapted from BVCA Academic Research Portal. https://www.bvca.co.uk/Research/Academic-Research-Portal.

3.3. DRY POWDER

Despite the differences between small, medium and large private equity funds, there has been an unprecedented flow of capital into them between 2012 and 2017. Among the buyout funds, the expansion has also revealed the challenge of "dry powder" in a context where heavy competition for deals puts upward pressure on asset prices and enhances the growth of megafunds.

One relevant trend reported by private equity funds is the gap between funds raised and equity invested- the so called capital "overhang". In 2007, private equity funds actually had a negative capital overhang of US$55 billion, meaning firms were investing more equity than they had raisen that year. Since then, however, the gap between funds raised and equity invested has widened significantly. This capital "overhang", according to Pitchbook Data, increased by more than US$141 billion during 2008 with the global economic crisis causing investment activity to decline by an estimated 60%. The trend to overhang has been mainly stimulated by liquidity-driven monetary policies.

Table 11 shows the largest PE firms by capital raised and dry powder in the last 10 years. The Luxembourg Private Equity & Venture Capital Association (LPVCA) points out that current dry powder amounted US$541 billion in 2017 (April) against US$473 billion in 2015-2016 and US$470 billion in 2006-2007. In this scenario, GPs can either overpay for assets or target lower quality assets. What LPVCA adds to our overview about fundraising and asset management is that competition for deals has grown. Besides, large and traditional investors are more careful in the selection of private equity funds.

Preqin (2018) data on alternative assets show that 92% of the investors said that they plan to allocate at least the same amount of capital to private equity in the coming 12 months, and 96% plan to maintain or increase those allocations over the longer term. It is worth noting that in the current PE industry, there are also "zombie funds", that is to say, buyout funds that raised their initial capital between 2003 and 2008 but has not raised capital since and hasn't executed a buyout deal since 2015. The Bain & Company

~(2018a) report identified 19 of these funds in North America and Europe
with more than 100 companies

**Table 11. Private equity firms: Capital raised and dry powder, last 10
Years, base 2017, in US$ billion**

PE firms	Headquarters	Capital Raised	Dry Powder
Carlyle Group	US	66.7	15.8
Blackstone Group	US	62.2	31.9
KKR	US	57.9	17.6
Goldman Sachs	US	55.6	16.0
Ardian	France	53.4	22.3
TPG	US	47.0	12.9
CVC Capital Partners	UK	42.2	10.6
Warburg Pincus	US	41.6	12.9
Advent International	US	40.9	14.4
Bain Capital	US	37.7	10.0

Source: Preqin apud Heberlein (2018). https://www.toptal.com/finance/private-equity-consultants/private-equity-industry.

3.4. PENSION FUNDS AND INSURANCE COMPANIES: THE SEARCH FOR ALTERNATIVE ASSETS

By 2020, the largest pools of pension fund assets are projected to remain concentrated in the US and Europe. In North America, pension fund assets reached US$19.3 trillion in 2012 and PwC estimates that by 2020, pension fund assets will rise by 5.7% a year to achieve over US$30 trillion of the US$56.5 trillion in total global. The PwC report, Asset *Management 2020: A Brave New World*, demographic changes, accelerating urbanization, technological innovations and shifts in economic power are reshaping the asset management trends where pension funds are relevant in global saving and investment. Three key factors seems to stimulate the global growth in assets: i) changes in government-incentivized or government-mandated retirement plans that will turn out to increase the use of defined contribution (DC) individual plans; ii) faster growth of high-net-worth-individuals in

South America, Asia, Africa and Middle East regions up to 2020; iii) the expansion of new sovereign wealth funds.

After the global crisis, quantitative easing policies expanded global liquidity, while the new near-zero interest rate setting inflated asset valuations and influenced financial investment strategies. Looking at Table 12, we can highlight that the annual performance of pension funds in the OECD area, over the last 15 years, between 2002 and 2017, the highest real average annual returns (net of investment expenses) were achieved in Canada (5.5%) and the Netherlands (5.3%).

As of 2017, the real investment rates of return (net of investment expenses) were above 5% in 22 in 12 out of the 60 reporting countries (Table 12). High positive results have been mainly associated to increasing equity prices among those countries where equities are relevant within pension assets: in 2017, the real net investment rate of return of Poland was 14.5%, followed by the United States (7.5%) and Australia (7.3%). Taking into account the real returns over the long-term perspective (15-years from December 2002-December 2017 and 10-years over December 2007 – December 2017), the average annual real net returns were positive in most of the OECD reported countries. Only four OECD countries presented a negative net return during this 10 year-period that covered the global financial crisis: Bulgaria (- 0.4%), the Czech Republic (- 0.1%), Estonia (- 1.3%) and the Slovak Republic (- 0.3%).

Regarding the asset-liability management of pension funds, it is worth noting that the continuity of liquidity-driven monetary policies and a decline in the long-term interest rates might affect the valuation of liabilities in a context where pension funds should have to redefine their asset strategies searching for higher real annual returns. Among other challenges, the adoption of austerity programs should be understood as a factor that negatively affected the evolution of pension systems.

Indeed, some key trends can be highlighted ten years after the global crisis: i) A shift to defined contribution (DC) pension plans, and ii) The increasing role of alternative assets, such as private equity funds, among pension assets.

Table 12. Pension funds: Returns over the last 5, 10 and 15 years, base 2017, selected OECD countries, in %

Average annual investment rates	Nominal			Real		
OECD countries/Period	5-year	10-year	15-year	5-year	10-year	15-year
Australia	9.6	4.9	6.7	7.5	2.5	4.2
Belgium	6.4	3.9	6.1	5.1	2.1	4.0
Canada	8.1	5.6	7.3	6.5	4.0	5.5
Denmark	5.3	5.8	6.3	4.6	4.4	4.7
Germany	4.0	3.9	4.1	2.9	2.6	2.6
Italy	3.5	3.0	3.7	3.0	1.7	2.0
Korea	3.5	4.0	4.1	2.3	1.8	1.6
Netherlands	7.1	6.0	6.9	6.0	4.4	5.3
Norway	7.0	5.3	6.7	4.6	3.2	4.7
Portugal	4.1	2.1	4.5	3.5	0.9	2.8
Switzerland	4.9	3.0	3.9	5.1	3.0	3.5
United States	5.7	2.1	3.9	4.2	0.5	1.7

Source: Madi (2018).
Note: Pension funds'returns refer to nominal and real average annual investment rates of return of pension assets, net of investment expenses.

Within the European region, many countries announced that they would need to make budget reductions in order to manage the public deficit soon after the 2008 crisis. At this respect, austerity measures concerning retirement rights and pensions in selected OECD countries that include cuts in public sector wages, cuts in social welfare, investment projects reduction, expenditure cuts and tax increases, changes in retirement age and pension payments (Pietras 2009). In truth, after the global crisis, many governments in OCDE countries have been committed to austerity programs, structural reforms in labour markets and a diversification of pension plans. According to OCDE (2018), in a mandatory pension plan: i) employers setup a plan for their employees, ii) employees contribute to a state funded pension scheme or iii) employees contribute to a private pension fund of their choice. In a quasi-mandatory, employers need to setup a pension plan as a result of labour agreements. In some countries, there are automatic enrolment programs at the national level where employees have the option to opt out of the plan under certain conditions.

In this setting, the PwC report warns that government-incentivized or government-mandated retirement plans privilege the expansion of defined contribution (DC) pension plans (such as the United States). In a defined contribution (DC) pension plan the employer, the employee or both make contributions on a regular basis in individual accounts. As matter of fact, the traditional occupational defined benefit (DB) pension plans have lost ground in many countries, such as Australia, Iceland, Israel, the Netherlands, Mexico, New Zealand, Sweden and the US. Broadbent et al. (2006) highlight that the shift to occupational defined contribution DC plans is associated with pension underfunding.

Table 13 aggregated data show the evolution of contributions and benefits as of 2017. Regarding the DB plans, lower discount rates used to value liabilities (as a result of quantitative easing policies) have been important factors to rethink the financial sustainability of pension funds. Besides, the increase in life expectancy result in longer periods of benefit payments to retirees for DB pension funds for a given retirement age (OECD 2017).

Ten years after the global crisis, the funding ratio of occupation defined benefit (DB) pension plans was below their pre-financial crisis levels in most of the OECD reporting countries. However, in Iceland, Indonesia, Mexico, the United Kingdom and the United State the funding ratio had already been below 100% for several years. Many factors drove the evolution of the funding ration and the asset- liability management of DB pension plans: low interest rates, composition of assets, number of members and wages, benefits paid, age structure of members, and aggregate price level. Therefore, the current main issue at stake is the path of evolution of benefits and contributions in different types of pension plans and how this evolution may affect the financial sustainability of pension funds. As a result, the search for higher profitability among alternative assets has been a commitment among pension funds' managers (Bradfors 2018).

Table 13. Defined benefit pension plans: Contributions and benefits, selected OECD countries, 2017, in %

OECD Countries	Contributions	Benefits
Luxembourg	37.1	- 6.8
New Zealand	18.3	- 23.3
Norway	8.4	- 3.6
Switzerland	8.3	- 5.0
Germany	7.7	- 5.0
Spain	5.6	- 7.9
Canada	5.2	- 5.4
Portugal	4.6	- 3.3
Indonesia	4.6	- 8.3
Belgium	4.0	- 2.8
Netherlands	3.9	- 3.3
Finland	2.5	- 3.5

Source: Madi (2018).

After the 2008 global crisis, pension funds' managers have been searching for alternative investments outside of traditional stocks and bonds, such as private equity investments. Between 2008 and 2017, most of pension funds in developed markets had expanded their alternative allocations from 7.2% of assets under management in 2008 to 11.8% in 2017, a 63% increase on average. In emerging markets, on average, pension funds increased their alternative investments from 0.97% in 2008 to 6.6% in 2017. Among the alternative asset investments, PE and real estate have been the most relevant (Ivashina and Lerner 2018). It is well remembering that, between 2008 and 2017, the policy of quantitative easing has been a driver of private equity deals and increasing asset prices in leveraged buyouts (LBOs) oriented to short-term returns. Indeed, Ivashina and Lerner (208) address that alternative investments have proven to be intensely controversial choices for pension funds because of the risk and liquidity commitments that should be matched to privilege the long-term horizons of pension funds. Pension funds report median net returns in their private equity allocations in the past 10 years ranging between 7.5% and 11.5%. This is well above the returns they obtained in the same period for fixed income, listed equity, hedge funds and even real estate (Preqin 2017a).

Pension funds are traditionally the most significant source of funding for private equity funds. Among the BVCA members, they committed 16% and 25% of the total funds raised to private equity in 2015 - despite the guidelines of prudential regulation. In Europe, the Institutions for Occupational Retirement Provision Directive (IORP) established a pan-European regulatory framework that set what pension funds may allocate to all alternative assets, including private equity, at most 30% of total assets. In April 2016, the Pan-European insurance and pensions regulator – EIOPA – recommended the adoption of common valuation rules and a standardised risk assessment to increase transparency in terms of risks and costs associated with investment decisions.

The search for alternative assets has also been a financial strategy in insurance companies committed to cope with the prudential treatment of private equity assets. Taking into account the European scenario, since 2016, Solvency II has been the prudential framework for insurance companies that outlines the methods for measuring and weighting risks so as to calculate capital requirements. For instance, the risk weight of 39% for private equity assets under the standard formula has been applied to AIFMD-authorised managers of AIFs that are closed-ended and unleveraged (EuVECAs are also subject to the same treatment). For BVCA members, insurance companies committed 9% and 5% of funds raised in 2015 and 2014, respectively. Only pension funds (public 30%, private 15%) and sovereign wealth funds (19%) are allocating more of their funds to PE today. In the long-term, 39% of all investors are planning to increase allocation to private equity- and only 5% plan to decrease. Today, insurance firms represent roughly 7% of private equity investors. The allocation of insurance firms to private equity has increased from 9% to 10% in the past 5 years.

As a matter of fact, the connection between pension funds and PE globalisation is one of the new features of the current era of financialization.

In: Private Equity Globalisation   ISBN: 978-1-53615-043-8
Editor: M. Madi   © 2019 Nova Science Publishers, Inc.

Chapter 4

PRIVATE EQUITY PORTFOLIO COMPANIES: INVESTMENT AND DIVESTMENT

4.1. PRIVATE EQUITY DEALS: TEN YEARS AFTER THE GLOBAL CRISIS

As highlighted by Bain & Company (2015), capital superabundance is the product of financial engineering, high-speed computing and a loosening of financial services regulations. As a result, global financial capital increased 53% from 2000 to 2010, reaching some US$600 trillion. In this scenario, private equity deals have been also increasing since the 2000s and their expansion has been considered a driver of the process of financialisation.

Before the 2008 global crisis, global liquidity enhanced PE fundraising and investments, while after the financial turmoil, three factors contribute that performance of private equity funds, mainly of the big-funds: difficulties to accomplish exit strategies, increasing refinancing needs and banks' liquidity management. Soon after the 2008 turmoil, the stabilization of financial markets fostered new PE deals. In the end, thanks to global liquidity, the rate of default amounted 6% among private equity firms between 2008 and 2013- accordingly Moody's.

Indeed, quantitative easing has been decisive to debt refinancing and, up to 2014, the PE industry has displayed resilience in a time characterized by slow global growth. After the 2008 financial crisis, many institutional investors revealed a growing interest in investing in PE funds. Therefore, institutional investors increased the levels of direct investing in a variety of ways, depending on the type of institution and its size, goals and comparative advantage as an investor. In mid-year 2014, the return for global buyout funds over a 10-year time horizon amounted 14.4%. As a result, the short-term returns on investment have been expected to be higher than the benchmark- the public equity markets.[1] Therefore, policies focused on quantitative easing stimulated the expansion of PE debt to the levels before the crisis. The new near-zero interest rate scenario has been decisive to refinancing private equity borrowers, inflate asset valuations and influenced the investment and exit strategies of private equity funds (Bain & Company 2014, 2).

Table 14. Private equity: Global deals, 2000-2017, selected years

Year	Global Deal volume (in US$ trillion)	Global Deal count (thousands)
2000	0.19	2.2
2005	0.56	4.2
2006	0.91	5.5
2007	1.40	7.3
2008	0.71	6.1
2009	0.30	4.1
2012	0.71	7.0
2014	1.04	8.4
2015	1.17	9.0
2016	1.11	8.8
2017	1.27	8.1

Source: McKinsey (2018).

---

[1] There is an index public market equivalent to compare private equity and public equity returns (Bain & Company 2015)

Indeed, prior to 2016, deal activity had been increasing. Ten years after the global crisis, the 2017 value of deals reached new records (Table 14). It is interesting to note that in 2017, the reduction of the global deal count can be associated with new trends: high competition for profitability deals, the increasing size of deals and the availability of low-cost debt. Table 14 shows some of the largest private equity-backed deals in 2017.

In the period between 2012 and 2017, despite the reduction in the number of transactions, the total value of deals has increased and the average deal size has been growing each year (Table 15). In this scenario, according to the Bain & Company (2018a) report, larger PE funds may behave like "corporations". An important advantage that corporations have these funds is related to the following aspects: i) corporations can extract strategic synergies from their acquisitions, making the value of these targets higher, and ii) corporations can do so over longer investment horizons. While private equity firms are looking for exits in the 5-10 year range, corporations in most cases simply hold their positions, allowing them to absorb higher valuation multiples on their acquisition targets. The result is that PE funds might reduce their market share in mergers and acquisitions to non-financial companies.

Table 15. Largest private equity deals, 2017

Portfolio company	Investment type	Location	Industry
Staples, Inc.	Public to Private	US	Retail
Belle International Holdings Limited	Public to Private	China	Retail
Stada Arzneimittel AG	PIPE - private investment in public equity	Germany	Pharmaceuticals
Nets Holding A/S	Public to Private	Denmark	Financial Services
West Corporation	Public to Private	US	Information Technology
PAREXEL International Corporation	Public to Private	US	Pharmaceuticals

Source: Preqin Private Equity Online.

As of 2017, countries like China, Korea and Japan were targets of private equity acquisitions, mainly in the following sectors: energy, information technology, home care and health services. In this scenario, one of the PE first reactions has been to privilege investment expansion through adds-on deals in order to obtain economies of scope and scale. Indeed, on behalf of high competition, PE buyout funds have searched for new opportunities to invest in late-stage (pre-IPO) technology firms with fast growth and high returns. In fact, some of the most well-known private tech - such as Uber, Airbnb, Spotify, and Pinterest - has received investments from large and traditional private equity groups. Other sectors like pharma and healthcare have also received investments. For instance, in the period between 2016 and 2017, Riverside Company bought New Jersey-based Dermatology Group, Hellman & Friedman acquired the provider of healthcare cost-management Multiplan and Blackstone acquired the physician services organization Team Health.

Also in 2018, technology companies continue to be attractive acquisition targets as private equity funds are requiring digital capabilities. Among other relevant sectors, LPEA (2018a) highlights healthcare, real estate and consumer products. Regarding the regional perspective, the PE activity in the US grew the most, increasing by 71% between 2017 and 2018, followed by Europe and Asia Pacific. Between April and September 2018, PE deals have been a crucial opportunity for enhancing strategic growth in a scenario of increasing competition and technological disruption. Great concerns arise in relation to the future interactions between private equity funds and small companies since their evolution might be deeply affected (Madi 2016).

Beyond financial engineering, the shift to new strategies, such like add-ons acquisitions, focuses on value creation through new operational strategies (Table 16). Many PE buyout funds prefer to invest into smaller companies within the same industries in their portfolios to realize strategic synergies (Brigl et al. 2016). Besides, private equity merging strategies also include the expansion in adjacent markets and industries. Recent evidence shows that buy and build deals can achieve the average internal rate of return (IRR) of 31.6% from entry to exit, a higher level when compared to the average IRR of 23.1% on buyout deals. Some significant recent examples of the "buy and build" strategy include: Kraft's acquisition of Heinz, where Berkshire Hathaway and 3G Capital were main investors; the acquisition of EMC by Dell that resulted in the largest private tech company in a deal where Silver Lake was a main investor.

According Table 16, an increased focus on portfolio management and operational improvements in the portfolio companies has become a critical tool for finding efficiencies. This is a shift from the focus on financial engineering that aimed to maximize returns for investors through leverage and the management of cash flows. Indeed, high competition and high valuations have been drivers of this shift. The Ernst & Young (2016) Private Equity Survey highlighted that LPs (investors) have been actively participating in the redefinition of the business model. Consequently, LPs have started to be directly interested in the sources of value creation in the PE portfolio companies, including growth of top lines and reduction of operational overhead. Therefore, in the current setting, private equity investors are no longer considered to be only a source of fundraising. As a result, LPs might turn out to be strategic partners and advisors within these companies.

4.2. EXIT CONDITIONS

Soon after of the 2008 global crisis, the lack of liquidity affected the exit scenario. However, after 2010, deal values started to grow and the highest global value of private equity backed-exits was observed in 2016 (Table 17) with a lower number of deals.

Among the key drivers that promoted the expansion of private equity investment, recent evidences show that:

- Low interest rates and cheap debt enhance the availability of money to invest.
- Expectations about outperformance in relation to public equity, real estate and fixed income investments foster PE deals.

- Mergers & acquisitions turn out to be an attractive path to growth since organic growth is difficult to achieve in a low-inflationary economy.
- Recycling of capital from mature investments is one important source of PE fundraising.
- High levels of liquidity in the portfolio of institutional investors are searching for alternative assets, such as PE investments.
- "Shadow capital" is looking at PE investments as co-sponsors and occasionally co-investors.

Table 16. Private equity acquisitions: Value of global buyouts and add-ons, 2005-2015, in US$ billion

Year	2005	2007	2008	2009	2011	2013	2015
Buyouts	2,154	2,917	2,264	1,384	1,973	1,934	1,721
Add-ons	864	1,441	1,244	779	1,397	1,131	1,637

Source: Dealogic apud Heberlein (2018). https://www.toptal.com/finance/private-equity-consultants/private-equity-industry.

Table 17. Global private equity backed-exits: Deal values, 2006-2017, in US$ billion

Year	Global Deal value (in US$billion)
2006	1,670
2008	1,505
2009	1,077
2010	1,813
2012	2,233
2014	2,841
2016	2,857
2017	2,475

Source: McKinsey (2018).

The key drivers that explained the performance of PE investments after 2010 started to put pressure on deal prices and holding periods. Indeed, the 3-5 year holding period seems to be over. After 2010, it might take longer to yield acceptable yields. Taking into account this scenario, private equity returns will decisively depend on overall macroeconomic conditions and on the implementation of operational improvements in a context where tax and regulatory innovations might dampen profitability. In short, in the PE scenario, the supply of profitable assets is limited and the value of deals is increasing. The value of deals is influenced by: expectation of future profits, liquidity preference and return of liquid assets relative to illiquid assets (Wray and Tymoigne 2008). Current competition between PE buyers has been pushing up the prices of the buyout deals since profitable assets are in limited supply. Indeed, the investment scenario is characterized by one of "hunt for deals" or "hunt for acquisitions". Besides, the availability of a greater amount of external funds boosts the state of expectations of borrowers and the reduction of the risk of borrowers puts further pressure on the prices of existing capital assets.

After 2014, deal value records have been observed in the US and Europe (LPEA 2018a). At the beginning of 2018, the US market continued to attract the majority of cross-border deals. Exit activity has been influenced by uncertainties and risks, although some IPOs have remained steady (in 2018 versus 2017) and with better valuations. From a regional perspective, while the US and Europe saw a decline in exits, the exit deals with IPOs in the Asia Pacific region increased substantially, mainly in China. Moreover, transactions in the secondary markets have been increasing as private equity firms seek ways to deploy dry powder. It is worth noting that, until 2004, secondary markets were still characterized by limited liquidity. Peterman and Lai (2009) estimated that the private secondary market grew from about US$4.4 billion in 1997 to about US$63 billion in 2007. Since then, secondary markets have been part of the PE portfolio management since companies can be sold before the target holding period. In this case, the sale of the portfolio company can be a tool for liquidity management.

Although the expansion of liquidity has played a key role in the GPs' ability to promote investment diversification, the current financial market scenario suggests challenges to GPs and LPs: higher returns might come at the expense of liquidity. According to Ernst & Young (2018) Global Corporate Divestment Study, divestments are at the core of companies' growth and strategies. The sales to strategic buyers have been the biggest channel for buyout-backed exits. In this context of uncertainties in relation to global expansion, corporations hold unprecedented cash reserves and more organic growth is hard to achieve. In this context, mergers and acquisitions are an attractive growth path and many PE portfolio companies are attractive goals

In short, the number of the 2017 private equity exits were lower than those observed in 2014-2016. Among the 2017 exit deals, Table 18 outlines the largest ones.

Taking into account different exit channels and geographies, North American buyout-backed exists were followed by European deals in value and number. In Asia-Pacific, GPs relied on the acquisition of minority stakes in companies. Table 19 outlines the main exit channels as of 2017.

Evidences from the current PE investment scenario show that expected returns are gradually being eroded while the limited supply of profitable assets put pressure on the value of deals in mergers and acquisitions. Nevertheless, as shown in Table 20, it seems like PE investments continue to outperform public markets around the world despite the recent challenges.

Table 18. Largest private equity exits, 2017

Portfolio company	Exit investment type	Location	Industry
Lightower Fiber Networks, LLC	Merger	US	Telecoms
Ista International GmbH	Buyout	Germany	Energy
West Corporation	Public to Private	US	Information Technology
WWR International	Buyout	US	Medical instruments
USI Holdings Corporation	Buyout	US	Insurance

Source: Preqin Private Equity Online.
Note: Completed deals.

Table 19. Private equity exit channels: Main findings, 2017

Exit channels	Characterisation	Performance/Examples as of 2017
Sales to strategic acquirers and other sponsors	This channel refers to transactions with strategic buyers that may be competitors, suppliers, or customers of the PE portfolio company.	The Anglo-Dutch company Unilever expanded its skin-care business in Asia where it paid US$2.7 billion for Carver Korea- a company controlled jointly by Bain Capital and Goldman Sachs since 2016. Crown Castle International almost doubled its wireless infrastructure business after buying LTS Group Holdings from Berkshire Partners, Ambry Partners, Pamlico Capital and HarbourVest in a deal that amounted to US$7.1 billion.
Sponsor-to-sponsor sales	This type of channel refers to secondary markets.	Leonard Green & Partners bought CPA Global - an intellectual property services company - from London's Cinven for US$3.1 billion.
IPO	An IPO typically makes up only a small portion of a PE firm's total stake in a company.	Global IPOs continue to be lower compared with the boom period from 2013 to 2015. In 2017, global IPOs and follow-on deals value amounted to US$129 billion. Follow-on deals value amounted to US$87 billion (67%) because of the stability of global markets, mainly in North America. However, in Europe, uncertainties about Brexit affected the exit performance.
Buyouts-Dividend recapitalizations.	This channel refers to a leveraged transaction.	Platinum Equity's US$4 billion leveraged buyout in network power business refers to Emerson Electric Co. and the company was subsequently renamed Vertiv.
Partial exits	This channel refers to the sale of a stake in a company—but keeping a hand in the business.	Relevant channel in 2017 since GPs are interested in extending holding periods. Berkshire Partners took a majority stake in Accela, a company that is a provider of government software solutions while the seller of Accela, Abry Partners, remained as investor. In other deal, Berkshire Partners sold a stake in Access- a company that is an information management services provider -to GI Partners while remained as a significant investor.

Source: Elaborated by the author. Adapted from Bain & Company (2018).

Maria Alejandra Madi

Table 20. Private equity buyout funds: Performance, as of June 2016

Investment Horizon	United States		Europe		Asia-Pacific	
In years	PE buyout funds	S&P 500 PME*	Developed Europe buyout funds	MSCI Europe PME	Asia-Pacific buyout and growth funds	MSCI Asua-Pacific PME
1	6	4	10	-11	2	-9
3	15	13	17	10	14	2
5	13	13	13	7	9	2
10	11	6	11	4	12	3
20	12	7	15	5	11	3

* Public Market Equivalents (PME).

Source: Heberlein (2018). https://www.toptal.com/finance/private-equity consultants/ private-equity-industry.

Note: Methodology based on Cambridge Associates (mPME). Performance in relation to public markets according to different investment horizons.

4.3. MANAGERIAL STRATEGIES AND PERFORMANCE

Table 21 outlines the main topics at stake in the debate on private equity governance, GPs strategies and practices to create value in the portfolio companies and agency problems within the PE industry.

In addition to the skills and performance of GPs, exit strategies have also been an important topic in current research. Exits are achieved through listing on the public markets in an initial public offering (IPO), selling to a strategic buyer (a trade sale or secondary buyout) or selling the company to the management (buy-back). Table 22 presents the results of recent research on acquisitions, valuations, share prices and different exit scenarios. Evidences compare PE performance over time and analyse the impacts of investments once the exit is completed.

Table 21. Private equity corporate governance: Literature review

Research results	References
Deal-level data from 395 PE transactions in West Europe, during the period 1991 to 2007, pointed out that the professional background of GPs and their skills impact on outperformance. Value creation strategies are well-succeeded by GPs with operational management skills while those with a financial background enhance successful M&A.	Acharya, Viral V., and Gottschalg, Oliver, Hahn, Moritz, and Kehoe, Conor. 2009. "Corporate Governance and Value Creation: Evidence from Private Equity. *European Corporate Governance Institute (ECGI) Finance Working Paper* No. 232.
20 executives in the UK who have been members of PE boards highlight the role of "leading" strategies through deep engagement with top management, almost complete alignment in objectives between executive and non-executive directors and access to financial information	Acharya, Viral V., Kehoe, Conor, and Reyner, Michael. 2009. "Private Equity vs. PLC Boards in the UK: A Comparison of Practices and Effectiveness." *ECGI Finance Working Paper* No. 233.
20 executives in the UK who have been members of PE boards highlight the role of "leading" strategies through deep engagement with top management, almost complete alignment in objectives between executive and non-executive directors and access to financial information.	Acharya, Viral V., Kehoe, Conor, and Reyner, Michael. 2009. "Private Equity vs. PLC Boards in the UK: A Comparison of Practices and Effectiveness." *ECGI Finance Working Paper* No. 233.
Operational changes in 103 restaurant chain buyouts, between 2002 and 2012, in Florida improved management after PE buyouts.	Bernstein, Shai and Sheen, Albert. 2013. "The Operational Consequences of Private Equity Buyouts: Evidence from the Restaurant Industry." *Standford University Working Paper*. Rock Center for Corporate Governance.
Although there is a diversity of management styles in PE companies, those GPs that hold an MBA in their background introduce more active strategies.	Bertrand, Marianne and Schoar, Antoinette. 2002. "Managing with Style: The Effect of Managers on Firm Policies." *MIT Sloan Working Paper* No. 4280-02.

Source: Elaborated by the author. Adapted from BVCA Research Academic Portal. https://www.bvca.co.uk/Research/Academic-Research-Portal/.

Table 22. Private equity exit strategies: Literature review

Research results	References
Considering a sample of 2,456 buyout transactions (including 448 secondary buyouts), there is no evidence that secondary buyouts generate lower equity returns.	Achleitner, Ann-Kristin, and Figge, Christian. 2014. "Private Equity Lemons? Evidence on Value Creation in Secondary Buyouts. *European Financial Management* 20 (2): 406-433.
98% of PE exits valuation show higher yields in buyouts deals after restructuring processes.	Hege, Ulrich, Lovo, Stefano, Slovin, Myron B., and Sushka, Marie E. 2018. "Divisional Buyouts by Private Equity and the Market for Divested Assets." *Journal of Corporate Finance* 53: 21-37.
PE firms exited through the secondary market can underperform those turned public (through IPOs) in the first three years after the exit.	Sousa, Miguel, and Jenkinson, Tim, 2013. "Keep Taking the Private Equity Medicine? How Operating Performance Differs between Secondary Deals and Companies that Go to Public Markets." *SSRN*. https://ssrn.com/abstract=2019595.
Among PE deals under financial pressure: i) buyers pay higher prices for the deals and use lower levels of debt, ii) sellers have shorter holding periods and sell the companies at lower prices. The bargaining power of each actor might influence the result of the PE exits.	Arcot, Sridhar, Fluck, Zsuzsanna, Gaspar, Jose-Miguel and Hege, Ulrich. 2015. "Fund Managers Under Pressure: Rationale and Determinants of Secondary Buyouts." *Journal of Financial Economics* 115(1): 102-135.
Although most private equity leveraged buyouts do not transfer value to investors and managers at the workers' expense. The relevance of regulation in the PE funds industry should be considered.	Bacon, Nick, Wright, Mike and Ball, Rod. 2013. "Private Equity, HRM and Employment." *Academy of Management Perspectives* 27(1): 7-21.
The source of acquisition financing is highly relevant to explain PE returns.	Bartlett, Robert P. 2008. "Taking Finance Seriously: How Debt-Financing Distorts Bidding Outcomes in Corporate Takeovers." *Fordham Law Review* 76.
PE buyouts from 2004 through 2010 relied on reputation to fill intentional contractual gaps. Both reputation and explicit contracting can play relevant roles in the management of private equity funds.	Cain, Matthew D., Davidoff Solomon, Steven, and Macias, Antonio J., 2012. "Broken Promises: The Role of Reputation in Private Equity Contracting and Strategic Default." *AFA 2012 Chicago Meetings*

Source: Elaborated by the author. Adapted from BVCA Academic Research Portal. https://www.bvca.co.uk/Research/Academic-Research-Portal.

Table 23. Private equity performance indicators: Literature review

Research results	References
From 1980 to 2005, US buyout funds have outperformed the S&P 500, despite cyclical variations, and money multiples seem to be better measures than IRRs.	Higson, Chris and Stucke, Rüdiger. 2012. "The Performance of Private Equity." *SSRN*. https://ssrn.com/abstract=2009067
PE outperformance is a compensation for a 10-year illiquid investment.	Ljungqvist, Alexander and Richardson, Matthew. 2003."The cash flow, return and risk characteristics of private equity." *NBER Working Paper* No. 9454.
Average PE buyout funds get higher results than the S&P 500. However, in comparison to small and value indices, the average PE buyout fund underperforms by an annual rate of -3.1%.	Phalippou, Ludovic. 2012. "Performance of Buyout Funds Revisited?." *Review of Finance*, 18 (1): 189–218.

Source: Elaborated by the author. Adapted from BVCA Academic Research Portal. https://www.bvca.co.uk/Research/Academic-Research-Portal.

Because of the specific features of private equity investments, academic literature has focused on performance indicators, PE performance against public markets. Table 23 outlines the main research results.

4.4. LIMITED PARTNERS SCRUTINY

According to Preqin (2017), the top five Limited Partners are:

1. CPP Investment Board (Canada), a public pension fund, with US$281 billion assets under management, and US$44.4 billion allocated to private equity;

2. Abu Dubai Investment Authority (United Arab Emirates), a sovereign wealth fund, with US$792 billion assets under management and US$39.6 billion allocated to private equity;

3. GIC (Singapore), a sovereign wealth fund, with US$350 billion assets under management, with US$31.5 billion allocated to private equity;

4. California Public Employees' Retirement System (US), a public
    pension fund, with US$305 billion assets under management and
    US$25.4 billion allocated to private equity; and
5. APG – All Pensions Group (Netherlands), asset manager, with
    US$432 billion assets under management and US$21.6 billion
    allocated to private equity.

Table 24. Private equity limited partners by type, 2016, in %

Limited Partners by type	Participation of each type of LP considering the Top 100 in the world, in %
Public Pension Fund	43
Asset manager	13
Insurance Company	13
Sovereign Wealth Fund	7
Endowment Plan	5
Private Sector Pesion Fund	5
Bank	3
Foundations	3
Others	8

Source: Preqin (2017b).
Note: Aggregate capital US$791bn.

Table 25. Private equity limited partners by region, 2016

Region	North America	West Europe	Far East	Middle East	Greater China	Australia	Nordic	Sub-Saharan
Number of LPs[*]	67	15	5	2	2	4	3	2
Total Allocation (US$ billion)	523	99	59	49	22	20	10	9

[*]Considering the largest 100 in the world.
Source: Preqin (2017b).

At the beginning of 2017, the main Limited Partners by type were
pension funds, asset managers and insurance companies (Table 24), while
the main geographic concentration was North America and Western Europe
(Table 25).

Preqin (2016) survey among Limited Partners on improvement achievements and challenges highlights that a significant number of private equity investors are: i) increasingly demanding lower management fees, ii) requiring more transparency from fund managers in reporting, iii) asking for a reduction of the amount of performance fees. Indeed, concerns about fairness in private equity business are relevant today, mainly related to the amount and scope of fees (Table 26). For instance, a US$2 billion fund that annually charges a 2% fee on assets under management results in a huge amount of GPs' earnings, regardless the performance of the portfolio companies. Besides, the absence of commitment of the GPs to disclosure information about business practices has enhanced new LPs´ strategies.

The demand for greater transparency has also generated in recent years a change in the type of investment vehicles chosen by LPs towards direct investments and co-investments. This innovation not only allows the LP participation in deals with GPs but also offers an alternative to reduce management fees. As a consequence of this change, LPs might start competing for deals against the PE managers themselves.

Table 26. Limited partners: Achievements and challenges related to private equity funds, June 2016, in proportion of respondents (%)

Items covered by the survey	Improvements achieved in the last 12 months	Improvements still required in the next 12 months
Management fees	39	66
Transparency at the PE Fund level	28	53
How performance fees are charged	28	53
Amount of performance fees	21	46
Manager commitment to the PE Fund	18	46
Lock-up period	2	16
Mininum rate of return	28	53

Source: Elaborated by the author. Adapted from Preqin (2016).

Table 27. Private equity performance:
Key drivers, literature review

Research results	References
In 238 funds, completed between 1993 and 2006, expected returns mostly result from revenue components not dependent on the industry performance.	Metrick, Andrew, and Yasuda, Ayako. 2009. "The Economics of Private Equity Funds." *Review of Financial Studies* 23: 2303-2341.
Evidences from 837 funds, from 1984-2010, show that there are agency problems that occur between investors and fund managers. While managers with higher fees deliver higher gross performance, agency problems are inevitable.	Robinson, David T., and Sensoy, Berk A. 2013. "Do Private Equity Fund Managers Earn Their Fees? Compensation, Ownership, and Cash Flow Performance." *The Review of Financial Studies* 26 (11): 2760-2797.
After LBOs, PE long-term returns relative to public counterparts might improve on behalf of i) higher involvement of sponsors, ii) CEOs' turnover independent from performance, iii) good information practices and effective monitoring.	Cornelli, Francesca and Karakaş, Oğuzhan. 2015. "CEO Turnover in LBOs: The Role of Boards." *IFA Working Paper*. London Business School.
PE manufacturing companies in Asia, Europe and the US are better managed than government, family and privately owned firms. Within 4,000 medium sized companies, this result depends on: i) human resources management, ii) operational practices focused on lean manufacturing, continuous improvement and monitoring.	Bloom, Nick, Sadun, Raffaella, and Van Reenen, John. 2009. "Do Private Equity Owned Firms Have Better Management Practices?" *Working Paper*, Centre for Economic Performance London School of Economics and Political Science.
Evidences consider the CEO turnover in formerly Communist countries between 1993 and 2010. PE firms' performance and exit strategies improve when the CEO turnover depends on the achievement of performance targets.	Cornelli, Francesca, Kominek, Zbigniew W., and Ljungqvist, Alexander. 2011. "Monitoring Managers: Does it Matter?." *NYU Working Paper* No. 2451/31350.
Analysing data from European companies in the period 2000 – 2008, financial distress risks seem to increase after PE buyouts although bankruptcy rates are not higher than those of non-private equity-backed companies.	Tereza Tykvová and Mariela Borell. "Do Private Equity Owners Increase Risk of Financial Distress and Bankruptcy?." 2012. *Discussion Paper* No. 11-076. Center for European Economic Research

Source: Elaborated by the author. Adapted from BVCA Academic Portal. https://www.bvca.co.uk/Research/Academic-Research-Portal.

Table 28. General partners' compensation: Literature review

Research results	References
Although incentive fees refer to a little part of total GPs'compensation, moral hazard and information agency problems are observed.	Ang, Andrew, and Sørensen, Morten. 2012. "Risks, Returns, and Optimal Holdings of Private Equity: A Survey of Existing Approaches." *Quarterly Journal of Finance* 2 (3).
Policymakers should uncover and fix the fundamental problem with carried interests in PE funds.	Field, Heather M., 2014. "The Real Problem with Carried Interests." *Hastings Law Journal*, 65 (2).
In terms of tax policy, there is the need to reconcile a progressive tax rate system to principles of distributive justice within the PE managers'compensation framework.	Fleischer, Victor. 2008. "Two and Twenty: Taxing Partnership Profits in Private Equity Funds." *New York University Law Review* 1.
The pay for performance - and the associated GPs fees - from future fund flows is higher than commonly discussed, mainly in PE buyout funds.	Chung, Ji-Woong, Sensoy, Berk A., Stern, L., and Weisbach, Michael S. 2012. "Pay for Performance from Future Fund Flows: The Case of Private Equity", *Review of Financial Studies* (11): 3259-3304.
After the acquisition, PE sponsors redesign contracts away from qualitative measures. Some subjective performance evaluation is generally used while vesting is not conditioned to market performance. Discussions about executive compensation reform are highlighted.	Cronqvist, Henrik and Fahlenbrach, Rüdiger. 2013. "CEO Contract Design: How Do Strong Principals Do It?." *Journal of Financial Economics* 108 (3): 659-674.
As PE portfolio companies do not invest differently than a matched sample of public control firms, there is no evidence of short-termism in management. However, debt investors and buyers of PE portfolio companies represent the two potential sources of wealth transfers.	Harford, Jarrad and Kolasinski, Adam C. 2014."Do Private Equity Sponsor Returns Result from Wealth Transfers and Short-Termism? Evidence from a Comprehensive Sample of Large Buyouts and Exit Outcomes." *Management Science* 60: 888-902.
Evidences from 837 funds, from 1984-2010, show that there are agency problems that occur between investors and fund managers.	Robinson, David T., and Sensoy, Berk A. 2013. "Do Private Equity Fund Managers Earn Their Fees? Compensation, Ownership, and Cash Flow Performance." *The Review of Financial Studies* 26 (11): 2760-2797.

Source: Elaborated by the author. Adapted from BVCA Academic Research Portal. https://www.bvca.co.uk/Research/Academic-Research-Portal.

It is worth noting that the American public pension funds are not able to participate in direct acquisitions. However, in Canada, the LP/GP competition included Canada's Public Pension Plan (CPPP) that in June 2015 acquired the General Electric arm named Antares. Other interested parties in the deal included the PE firms Apollo Management and Ares Capital, besides Mitsubishi Bank.

LPs are also increasingly concerned about the level of GPs' commitment of all assets under management on the funds. In the Ernst & Young (2016) Global Private Equity Fund and Investor Survey, 73% of investors believe that GPs should have at least a 3% commitment of all assets on the funds, while almost half of those respondents prefer a level of GPs´ commitments above 5% of all assets under management. Indeed, LPs expect that GPs could enlarge their participation in the funds and, therefore, reduce their reliance on management fees and privilege the portfolio performance. According to Preqin (2016), in 56% of cases, the level of GPs' commitments of all assets was less than 3% during 2014.

In the private equity current scenario, there is a controversy about the relative importance of the key performance drivers. In short the main issue at stake is: *does PE performance emerge from value creation or from financial engineering?* Table 27 outlines some of the main positions in the debate.

Among the concerns about fees, one related discussion is about management fees and the GPs' strategies towards long-term performance of private equity investments. Table 28 outlines a literature review on the debate around the management fees.

Indeed, some scholars agree that private equity governance is the key driver of value creation where leverage has a relevant role. Other scholars point out potential negative effects of leveraged strategies at the core of the business model that has historically been focused on financial engineering. Policy concerns arise on behalf of excessive debt and systemic risks posed by buyout transactions. Other controversial issue at stake is short-termism in private equity business.

In: Private Equity Globalisation   ISBN: 978-1-53615-043-8
Editor: M. Madi   © 2019 Nova Science Publishers, Inc.

Chapter 5

PRIVATE EQUITY BUSINESS AND LABOUR

5.1. CHANGING BUSINESS MODELS AND WORKING CONDITIONS

Economic conditions are constantly changing. Today, our generation is confronted with the outcomes of contemporary globalisation that is a broader, complex, and multifaceted process characterized by new markets, new actors and new rules. Indeed, globalisation has produced many changes in our economy, society, culture, and politics. As a result, deep pressures to conform to new standards of behaviour, such as efficiency and competitive performance, have forced individuals and communities not only to rethink values and practices but also to rebalance tradition and change.

In the scenario of globalized markets, individuals and communities face many challenges to be resilient because of deep changes in markets, wealth and power. Throughout the last forty years, most governments around the world supported the long-run process of neo-liberal reforms that turned out to be characterized by the financialisation of the capitalist economy. By negatively influencing labour and working conditions, it rendered increasingly difficult to reach (or even approach) the level of full employment. In this setting, changes in corporate ownership, through waves of mergers and acquisitions, created new business models where companies, while highly powerful and concentrated, are managed as financial assets and liabilities to be traded (Madi 2017).

Globalisation has also enhanced great changes in worldwide production, in particular the shift of manufacturing to Asia-Pacific countries and the resulting imbalances of global trade. In this context, developed countries have imposed a trade and financial liberalisation agenda on developing countries through the global governance of the multilateral institutions, such as the International Monetary Fund, World Bank and the World Trade Organisation. This fact has been particularly noticeable in Latin America and Africa where neoliberal policies have been implemented more thoroughly than in Asia. Nevertheless, in all regions, the overall effects of financialisation at the local levels shaped new articulations between the economic and social spheres overwhelmed by political tensions.

Taking into account the labour markets, employability seems to be configured by private strategies that aim at cost reduction, labour flexibility and efficiency targets. Indeed, the current dynamics of labour markets puts pressure on the vulnerability of workers, mainly young people, and on the expansion of precarious jobs. Therefore, job instability and fragile conditions of social protection enhance the redefinition of survival strategies. Consequently, workers turned out to redefine their skills, become informal entrepreneurs or migrate, among other examples of the current worldwide transformations.

In this setting, current neoliberal policies of resilience have been increasingly prevalent in current economic thinking and policies. The policy recommendations seek to foster the capacity of individuals and communities to cope with market uncertainties. Brasset and Holmes (2016) present a literature review on the neoliberal (and managerial) policies of resilience, characterized as a set of governance techniques aimed to manage uncertainty and achieve the adaptation of individuals and communities to global changes. Considering the labour markets, for example, the neoliberal policies of resilience have turned out to enhance the workers' adaptation to the "market discipline" and, therefore, there has been a re-distribution of the responsibilities among the state, businessmen, investors and workers. As a consequence, the evolution of unemployment results from the "unsuitable" or "inappropriate" behaviour of workers to face a changing real-world.

As a matter of fact, in the frame of the neoliberal policies of resilience, human life turns out to be focused on the attempt to face exogenous uncertainties and risks in order to create adaptive strategies. In short, the sole purpose of resilient individuals and communities seems to be survivability. Indeed, in the light of current global social and political challenges. The spread of the discourse of resilience calls for a critical reflection on the failures of economic thinking and economic policies.

Competitive forces and technological disruptions have been drivers of changes in firms, work and workplace. Today, the working conditions are increasingly dependent on complex cognitive processes, team-based activities, social skills and technological competence. While organizations have become less hierarchical, precarious jobs have increased (Standing 2011). The enterprise model introduced by Toyota in the 1970s provoked changes in organizations across the globe, mainly in manufacturing and product development. The key principles to reduce cycle time, develop mass customization processes and support continual innovation are: i) customer's needs and preferences, ii) the identification of the value chain, iii) the elimination of non-value added activities, iv) the reduction of inefficiencies.

Indeed, we are living in a labour-saving context. Access to internet services enabled the transformation of traditional work under Fordism, to knowledge work, characteristic of post-Fordism. Against the old centralized large corporation, e.g., General Motors, current communication channels and employment practices have been redefined in a context of changing remuneration and payment practices task rotation, multi-skilling and team work. Potential consequences include fragmentation of work, crowdsourcing and virtualization of work.

Technological change has significantly transformed the labour scenario as the result of the diffusion of innovative practices at the micro-level. Technological change has already significantly transformed the labour market on behalf of the diffusion of innovative practices at the micro-level. Crowdsourcing, for example, is the outsourcing of tasks to a large, undefined group of people in an open call. Current challenges in working conditions are also related to the emergence of a crowd of freelancers available and able to quickly do the necessary tasks. The cloud based work is characterized by on-demand services (Ipeirotis 2012). Low wages, lack of rights, unprotected jobs, increasing informality are the hidden side of cloud workers.

In fact, the deleterious social outcomes of the ongoing business strategies have become a constant feature of today's global and financialised economy (Blum 2008). Indeed, in the current context of "institutionalized short-termism", changing working conditions result from:

- continuous restructuring of companies to generate cash outflow,
- redefinition of workers' tasks,
- increased outsourcing and casualization to cut costs,
- sell-offs and closures of plants regardless of productivity and profitability,
- deteriorating working conditions in the workplace,
- more control on workers,
- diminished employment security.

At this respect, David Weil´s 2014 book, *The Fissured Workplace*, highlights that nowadays the employer-worker relationship has been submitted to delivering value to investors. As Weil's groundbreaking analysis shows, the result has been an ever-widening income inequality. It is in this complex labour scenario that private equity funds turned out to be major global employers (Table 29).

Today, each one of the PE firms Carlyle and KKR employs, for instance, almost 700,000 people in their portfolio companies, while Blackstone has around 600,000 employees (LPEA 2018). Apollo has 300,000 workers in its portfolio companies, while Warburg Pincus, General Atlantic and TPG have a slightly smaller amount of employees. It is worth remembering that in the corporate sector, the top employers are Wallmart with more than 2 million employees, China National Petroleum with almost 1.5 million employees), and China Post Group with nearly 1 million workers, according to Statista (2019).

In his deep social and cultural analysis of globalisation, the well-known sociologist Zygmunt Bauman (2000, 122) stated: "The downsizing obsession is, as it happens, an undetachable complement of the merger mania. It is the blend of merger and downsizing strategies that offers capital and financial power the space to move and move quickly, making the scope of its travel even more global, while at the same time depriving labour of its own bargaining and nuisance-making power, immobilizing it and tying its hands even more firmly".

Following Bauman, we can say that financial power and the private equity business model are interrelated. Capital mobility, liquid strategies and behaviours, financial speculation, mergers and acquisitions have submitted livelihoods to huge losses in terms of unemployment, working conditions, workers' rights and income distribution. The outcomes were not socially acceptable since the restructuring programs have put pressure on social and economic protections for all workers. Therefore, the apprehension of the dynamics of high finance is decisive to improve the understanding of the social impacts of business strategies in contemporary capitalism. As investors prefer short-term results, the reorganization of business and markets has turned out to increase social vulnerability.

Table 29. Private equity firms:
Total employment in the top five, 2016

Country/Region	Total Employment
United States	960,231
Europe	911,896
Asia-Pacific	878,476

Source: Hammoud et al. (2017). https://www.bcg.com/enca/publications/2017/value-creation-strategy-capitalizing-on-new-golden-age-private-equity.aspx.

At the heart of Bauman´s argument is that the capital accumulation process and the *merger mania* involve *social* relations driven by profit and competition. At this respect, Bauman (2000, 147) addressed: "Flexibility is the slogan of the day, and when applied to the labour market it augurs an end to the " job as we know it", announcing instead the advent of work on short-term contracts, rolling contracts or no contracts, positions with no in-built security but the "until further notice" clause. Working life is saturated with uncertainty".

What the philosopher adds to our understanding about the real-world working conditions is that business liquid strategies shape a social dynamics where the search for flexibility is supported by a kind of rationale that reinforces short-termism.

Indeed, in spite of the euphemisms rationalization and *capital flexibility*, finance regulates the pace of investment and the process of adjustment of the labour force. Workers are fired on behalf of the short-term profit targets and those who remained are responsible for carrying the burden by increasing productivity. In the context of *labour flexibility*, workers cannot easily face all the deep changes that are happening in their workplaces. Therefore, the outcomes of the strategies based on *rationalization* and *flexibility* turned out to have increased uncertainty in livelihoods.

5.2. PRIVATE EQUITY FUNDS AS EMPLOYERS

The expansion of private equity funds opens up novel ways of framing the evolving relation between labour and capital. As Keynes highlighted in his approach to employment in a monetary economy of production this economy is based on the asymmetrical (hierarchical) relationship between firms and workers (Gnos 2006). Keynes constructed the principle of effective demand in line with his conception that entrepreneurs/managers make decision about the levels of employment with reference to the demand they expect for their output.

In the aftermath of the global crisis, quantitative easing failed to restore the creation of jobs (Rochon and Rossi 2013, 211). Indeed, although quantitative easing avoided PE funds' default, this policy has been a driver of high competition and increasing value deals. Considering the labour costs in the PE business model, new strategies aim to reduce the expensive workforce by substituting capital for labour, particularly as sophisticated robotic penetrates traditional services business like food and healthcare.

New telecommunications and information technology can also increase the utilization of teleworking, outsourcing and crowdsourcing.

So far, the outcomes of the role of private equity funds as employers has been controversial. Some managerial reports consider leveraged buyouts as a revolution in corporate ownership on behalf of the creation of new assets, funding options and governance structures. Jensen (1989), for instance, argues that the private equity funds' business model may improve corporate performance. Many factors have been assessed to justify takeovers: increase in profitability, cost reduction, tax gains, management efficiency and cost of capital reduction (Kaplan 1989; Smith 1990; Ross et al. 1999). After the takeovers, Shapiro and Pham (2008) pointed out positive outcomes of private equity strategies in the UK and US in terms of productivity and employment. In 2018, for instance, the Luxembourg Equity Private Association highlighted the successful development of Burger King and Quick fast-food transactions led by Kharis Capital in creating a huge number of jobs for the real economy.

However, global trade unions have been addressing an unfavorable perspective since private equity globalisation expresses the power of centralized money to configure labour conditions while rationalization strategies put further pressure on working conditions (IUF 2007).

Table 30 outlines further research results about the controversial features of labour relations under the private equity business model.

The literature review shows that while some scholars criticize the private equity business model on behalf of low wages and productivity, other researchers argue that investments in the portfolio firms enhance the growth of production and job creation. Indeed, this debate is far from having been concluded.

In order to add more information to this debate, the outcomes of private equity strategies and practices in the UK are presented in Table 31. The UK 2017 survey showed a high percentage of lower salary jobs in the PE portfolio companies versus the private sector. Besides, the large number of part-time jobs in the portfolio companies has been associated with the mix of sectorial investments that created 77% of jobs in consumer services (such as, restaurants) and healthcare (such as, home cares). Zero-hours contracts are also typical in the healthcare sector.

Table 30. Private equity and labour relations: Literature review

Research results	References
After PE acquisitions, workforce skills improve in a context of technological change.	Agrawal, Ashwini and Tambe, Prasanna. 2016. "Private Equity and Workers' Career Paths: The Role of Technological Change." *The Review of Financial Studies* 29 (9): 2455–2489.
Over the period 1999-2004, the effects of PE buyouts (1,350 leveraged buyouts) were not significant on employment growth but have low effects on wage growth than non-leverage buyouts.	Amess, Kevin and Wright, Mike. 2007. "The Wage and Employment Effects of Leveraged Buyouts in the UK." *International Journal of the Economics of Business* 14(2).
Research results based on 839 French deals contrast evidences that LBO targets invest less or downsize.	Boucly, Quentin, Sraer, David Alexandre, and Thesmar, David. 2011. "Growth LBOs". *Journal of Financial Economics* 102: 432–453.
Considering the US private equity deals from 1980 to 2005 (regarding 3,200 target firms with 150,000 establishments), PE strategies had more impact on job reallocation than on net job creation.	Davis, Steven J., Haltiwanger, John C., Jarmin, Ron S., Lerner, Josh and Miranda, Javier, 2011. "Private Equity and Employment". *Chicago Booth Research Paper* No. 11-31.
Taking into account a group of developed economies, there is no evidence that PE investment significantly boosts employment, productivity or growth at the macroeconomic level.	Ellis, Collin. 2009. "The Economic Impact of Private Equity: what we know and what we would like to know." *Journal Venture Capital* 11(1).
PE leveraged buy-outs (LBOs) in the UK provoked a significant decrease in employment levels in acquired firms in the year immediately after the acquisition. The downsizing observed has not been effective either to increase productivity or to shape a clearer focus in business strategies.	Goergen, Marc, O'Sullivan, Noel and Wood, Geoffrey. 2011. "Private Equity Takeovers and Employment in the UK: Some Empirical Evidence." *ECGI - Finance Working Paper* No. 310.
Across private equity buyouts in the US, the sample of target companies has not created jobs between 1980 and 2005.	Montgomerie, J. 2008. "Labour and the Locusts: Private Equity's Impact on the Economy and the Labour Market." *Conference Report of the Seventh British-German Trades Union Forum*, London: Anglo-German Foundation for the Study of Industrial Society

Research results	References
Rationalization strategies reduced the employment levels in PE leveraged buyouts for more than 3 years after the acquisition.	Davis, S., Haltiwanger, J., Jarmin, R., Lerner, J., and Miranda, J. 2008. "Private Equity and Employment." *Working Papers* 08-07, Center for Economic Studies, US Census Bureau.
Across 36,000 UK manufacturing establishments, better PE portfolio companies' performance was due to outsourcing.	Cressy, R., Munari, F., and Malipiero, A. 2007. "Creative destruction? UK Evidence that buyouts cut jobs to raise returns." *Working Paper Series. SSRN.* http://ssrn.com/abstract=1030830
Working conditions in a variety of industries have been reconfigured after private equity deals: fewer jobs, lower wages and pensions, rising inequality and a huge increase in "moral hazard".	Harris, R, Siege, D. S., Wright, M. 2005. "Assessing the impact of management buyouts on economic efficiency: plant-level evidence from the United Kingdom." *The Review of Economics and Statistics* 87(1): 148-153.
Employment reduction, lower workers' income and productivity challenges were observed in companies after PE buyouts.	Appelbaum, E., and Batt, R. 2014. *Private Equity at Work: When Wall Street Manages Main Street.* United States: Russell Sage Foundation.

Source: Elaborated by the author. Adapted partially from BVCA Academic Research Portal. https://www.bvca.co.uk/Research/Academic-Research-Portal/Employment.

Table 31. Private equity portfolio companies: Employment, wages and human resource management, UK, 2016

Topics	Main results from the survey
Holding period	• 4.2 years from initial acquisition to exit.
Job creation	• Employment has annually grown by 2.6% • Organic employment growth slowed in 2016 and was lower than the UK private sector benchmark.
Employment costs and benefits	• Average annual employee compensation growth at 3.5% is above the UK private sector benchmark at 2.5%. • Average employment cost annual growth was 4.6% in 2016, above the the UK private sector benchmark of 2.3%. • Almost half of the jobs are for part-time work with annual compensation lower than £12,500 - proportion that is higher in relation to public companies. • 5.2% of jobs are on zero-hours contracts, slightly below the UK benchmark of 5.5%. • Regarding pension plans, there have been changes to defined benefit (DB) pension schemes and the aggregated value of liabilities of DB schemes exceeds the value of assets.

Table 31. (Continued)

Topics	Main results from the survey
Operating capital and capital expenditures	• The longer-term pattern of operating capital employed rate growth has been variable. 48% of the current portfolio companies have made net bolt-on acquisitions. Free cash flow and debt have been the sources of operating capital.
Operating capital and capital expenditures	• Growth in capital expenditure was strong in the years following the downturn, but since 2014 investments on R&D has declined. In aggregate, companies have annually grown operating capital employed by 2.3% during the holding period while the rate of the public company benchmark was 4.2% in the same period. • GPs have greater control of working capital in the portfolio companies.
Labour and capital productivity	• Annual growth in labour productivity in the portfolio companies at between 1.6% and 1.8% is broadly aligned to public company and economy-wide benchmarks. • Increases in capital productivity exceeded public company benchmarks • The revenue growth from existing investments differs from public company revenue growth centered on new capital employed.

Source: Elaborated by the author. Adapted from BVCA (2017).
Note: The BVCA survey includes 44 private equity portfolio companies.

5.3. GENDER DIVERSITY

The roots of gender and poverty studies began with Pearce (1978) who coined the expression 'feminization of poverty'. The author considered female-headed families, excluding poor women who live in male- headed families, based on the argument that the proportion of families headed by women among the poor has been increasing since the 1950s. In her opinion, women have become poorer because of their gender.

The recent dynamics of the global labour market has reinforced the precariousness of women's employment and working conditions. Indeed, although women have been increasing their participation rate in the last decades, they worked in more precarious occupations. Indeed, women's participation is stronger in the services sector where working hours are longer and wages lower. In addition to the wage gap (globally, women earn

77% of what men earn), unpaid work could also be an extra onus on women. The increasing weight of unpaid work is more likely when women become unemployed and return to their homes and take more responsibility for housework than men, or because the loss of family income makes it impossible to support the remuneration of domestic workers. Within the United Nations goals, gender equality is required for eradicating poverty. Indeed, the "vicious circle" of impoverishment could be surmounted if policy makers rethink employment and income policies under a gender approach.

Table 32. Women at work: UK private equity industry, 2018

Topics	Main findings
Overall participation	• Women are underrepresented in private equity. Evidence of 178 firms with almost 5,000 employees shows that women comprise just 29% of the private equity workforce. By comparison women comprise 48% of the UK labour force.
Non–investment roles	• There is a much stronger representation of women in non-investment roles, where they comprise 60% of the workforce.
Investment teams	• Women are significantly underrepresented in investment teams. Only 14% of investment professionals are women. • Women represent just 6% of senior roles in investment teams. More women work at the mid and junior level, with 15% of the mid-level roles (Directors, Principals, VPs, etc.) and 27% of the junior roles (Associates, Analysts, etc.). • More than a quarter of the firms have no women in their investment teams. In firms with 10 or fewer employees 67% of the teams are comprised entirely of men. However, firms with over 80 employees have no "male-only" teams • In larger firms, more women work in investment teams at all levels while senior female representation at small and medium sized firms is only 4%. • More junior to mid women take part of investment teams in all firms regardless of size. In firms with over 80 employees, women represent 31% of junior investment roles.
Smaller firms	• Overall, women comprise 29% of private equity industry employees. • There is greater representation of women in smaller firms. • In firms with 10 employees or fewer, women represent 31% of the total. In firms with 11 to 25 employees, and in firms with 26 to 80, women represent 29%. This number drops to 26% in firms with over 80 employees.

Source: Elaborated by the author. Adapted from BVCA (2018).

Table 33. Women at work: UK venture capital industry, 2017

Topics	Main findings
Overall participation	• Women are underrepresented in UK venture capital. • Women comprise just 27% of the venture capital workforce in the U.K, against 47% of the UK labour force.
Investment teams	• Women are significantly underrepresented in investment teams. • Only 18% of investment professionals are women. In non-investment roles, women comprise 43% of the workforce.
Investment decision-making	• Women represent just 13% of decision makers. • In junior and mid-levels there are fewer women than men.
Larger firms	• Larger firms have a higher ratio of women employees. • Overall, women comprise 27% of venture capital industry employees. • There is greater representation of women in larger firms than in smaller firms.
Lack of representation	• Almost half of all firms have no women in their investment teams. • Investment teams with 11-15 employees have particularly poor representation of women. • There are fewer decision making women in teams comprising 11-15 employees.
Comparison with US	• Considering investment teams, 11% of US decision makers are women – 2% behind the UK. • 45% of all employees in US venture capital firms are women, which is 18% ahead of the UK.
Comparison with entrepreneurial and digital industries	• The UK's venture capital and digital industries have 27% women workers. • However, the venture capital industry lags behind early-stage entrepreneurial businesses based in the UK by 6%.

Source: Elaborated by the author. Adapted from DIVERSITY VC and BVCA (2017). http://www.diversity.vc/women-in-uk-vc/.

5.4. GLOBAL CAPITAL AND TRADE UNIONS

The expansion of the organization of production across different nation-states has been a reality since the middle 1950s. The existence of nation-states with different regulatory regimes in labour markets, social security, financial and fiscal regulations have created opportunities for specific strategies offered by transnationality. *Who are the key economic actors holding the largest fraction of control? To what degree are the top economic actors interconnected?*

To answer these questions, James Glattfelder analysed the global ownership network of transnational corporations (TNCs) in his 2012 book *Decoding Complexity: Uncovering Patterns in Economic Networks.* The author uncovers the true organization of key global actors and novel features of complex systems of current real-world ownership networks. His effort lies at the interface between the realms of economics and the emerging field loosely referred to as complexity science.

Among his research conclusions, Glattfelder lists the top 50 corporate power-holders as relevant economic actors. As a matter of fact, these actors are highly interconnected and organize a global network of corporations. Another interesting observation is that most of the top power-holders are financial intermediaries.

From an economic point of view, these findings may suggest new questions because of their implications on market competition and financial instability. The global network of interactions enhances systemic risks since companies have potentially wide influence on investment, production and employment at the local levels. As the interests of private companies do not generally coincide with the interests of society as a whole, these risks need to be dealt with new anti-trust practices and new rules on cross-ownerships among corporations.

As Grazia Ietto-Gillies (2011) highlights the understanding of modern economies cannot be arrived at without an understanding of how transnational corporations (TNCs) operate. At the micro level, strategic behaviour and bargaining power – particularly in relation to workers and governments – should be analysed. Among macro issues, policies could minimize the effects of TNCs' activities for economies and societies. Indeed, as Ietto-Gillies claims "TNCs are here to stay"- and we can add - "Private equity funds are here to stay". Indeed, any fruitful attempt to understand contemporary capitalism should include TNCs and private equity funds as major institutions with an outstanding position in a global network that affect workers and countries.

Indeed, in the global network of the PE business, companies are viewed as a set of assets that has to be bought or sold in order to pursuit short-term profits. While current corporate governance focuses on publicly traded companies, it has generally weaker requirements for unlisted companies. The report *Workers' Guide to Private Equity Buyouts* summarizes the concerns about the path of private equity governance that has historically privileged a short-term perspective: "Private equity firms buy a company as a financial asset with the potential to generate an instant cash flow to the new owners in the short-term. Huge returns are generated through aggressive restructuring to cut costs and by financial reengineering based on large quantities of debt." (IUF 2007,10)

The PE business model has favored downsizing and cost reduction against job creation. As a matter of fact, as labour costs are frequently considered large expense items, the GPs tightly manage those costs. In fact, the social consequences of the rationalization strategies have been less explored by academic researchers, while extensive studies have been developed by private sector companies and industry bodies that tend to report only success stories (Cressy et al. 2007b). Under rationalization strategies, managers foster: i) turnover, ii) accelerated cost cutting through layoffs, closures, outsourcing, iii) further reductions in productive investment and R&D, iv) increased pressure on collective bargaining power, v) casualization, and vi) capping or closing pensions (IUF 2008). Indeed, financial strategies are at the core of the leveraged buyout business model adding significant pressures on workers and trade unions.

Before the 2008 global crisis, metalworkers and their unions have built and increasingly implemented strategies to counteract the potential excesses of leveraged buyouts and to protect the interests of workers and their communities. Collective bargaining is one of the key issues, together with the mobilization of workers and the cooperating among trade unions and social allies, nationally and internationally, in the fight for regulations that safeguard public interest, support quality employment and generate productive jobs. Affiliates of the International Metalworkers' Federation (IMF) have developed and increasingly used counterstrategies through collective bargaining to defend employment and working conditions, to maintain pensions and secure investments, and to influence conditions of potential leveraged buyouts. These approaches have evolved over time as trade unions carefully account for institutional and legal factors in order to enhance their effectiveness (Blum 2008). For instance, examples from the automotive, aerospace and mechanical engineering industries reveal trade unions' practices and challenges:

1. Unite in the UK set out concrete demands to condition the sale by Ford of Jaguar and Land Rover, impacting the decision of the eventual buyer among which were auto assembler companies and some private equity funds. Among the range of important guarantees achieved in the conditions of sale to Tata Motors in 2008, was the continuation of existing arrangements for trade union recognition and bargaining, protection of workforce terms and conditions of employment including current pension arrangements, and long-term production, development, investment and sourcing commitments from Ford and Tata.

2. With the acquisition by Cerberus of Chrysler in 2007, in which Daimler retained a 20% stake, the United Auto Workers (UAW), Canadian Auto Workers (CAW) along with IG Metall insisted that the new ownership and company structure should contribute to a safe and sustainable future for the Chrysler Group. Industry and company level collective bargaining by the UAW and CAW have ensured continuity of negotiated protections of workforce terms and conditions of employment including pension and healthcare provisions.

3. In addition, on behalf of Dana´s financial problems in the US, in 2006, the company tried to cancel labour contracts and the UAW

and United Steel Workers (USW) together made it clear that such drastic action could result in a labour dispute (Blum 2008). The high-stakes bargaining led to a successful outcome, which included involvement by Centerbridge, a private equity investor. The company agreed: i) to limit how much debt the company could take on, ii) to regular meetings and reports regarding cash-flows, and iii) to expand the rights of unorganised Dana workers. The unions insisted on fair procedures, including card-check recognition, a process where employers agree to recognise a union once a majority of workers indicate their preference by signing union authorisation cards.

4. Commercial aircraft facilities spun off from Boeing in 2004 formed Spirit AeroSystems. The International Association of Machinists (IAM) and UAW negotiated the Union Equity Program. As a result, workers were given shares that would provide to them benefits from future growth, and rehire and recall provisions to cover nearly all fellow union members. When the company was brought to the market, the value of the shares for workers more than made up for the prior wage concessions, generating an average of US$61,000 per worker through early 2007 (Blum, 2008).

In addition to these actions, trade unions have been working with OECD Ministers and G8 leaders to promote a regulatory taskforce on private equity (Tate 2007). After the financial crisis, the demand for financial regulation has been stressed by global unions that also warned about the interconnections between the private equity debt structure and global systemic risks (Industry all Global Union 2011). Financial regulation should break up those financial institutions "too big to fail", implement controls over the non-bank shadow financial economy, such as private equity firms, and eliminate tax and regulatory havens. As of September 2011, with the prospect of increasing unemployment because of the global economic downturn, trade unions urge for changes in policy making to overcome the effects of austerity. Among the main global trade unions, the International Metalworkers' Federation, the International Trade Union Confederation

(ITUC) and the Trade Union Advisory Committee to the OECD (TUAC), demanded action and policy changes in global governance.

Table 34. Global trade unions: Asking for reforms

Topics	Detailed proposals
Transparency	• Transparency in formal levels of disclosure, prudential rules and risk management. • Transparency and reporting in performance, risk management and fee structure. • Transparency in financial accounts and executive rewards.
Business plan	PE portfolio companies should elaborate business plans including information about: • Working conditions. • Investment plans and innovations. • Plans for selloffs/closures. • Exit strategies.
Tax regulation	• Tax deductibility of debt service. • Tax on capital gains and tax havens. • Specific tax on the activities of private equity funds (e.g., Denmark).
Corporate Governance	New regulations on corporate governance should include: • Measures to discourage short-termism in the business targets. • Greater transparency and public reporting requirements. • More supervision and oversight by public authorities.
Corporate Governance	• Limits to the levels of leverage and taxation on capital gains after the sale of PE assets. • Enforcement of the obligations of private equity funds with respect to all relevant employer obligations.
Financial Stability	• Management of systematic risk through: • Revision of leverage practices. • Improvement of the reporting procedures. • Rating of PE portfolio companies. • Reform of regulatory agencies, such as the role of central banks in the shadow banking system. • Open information to all the stakeholders.

Source: Elaborated by the author. Adapted from ITUC (2007) and Amicus (2007).

Global unions addressed the relevance of job creation measures led by infrastructure programs, health care, education, and climate-related investments. In this agenda, progressive tax measures and financial transactions tax could help to reduce the public deficit and to improve income distributions.

Indeed, global trade unions have been active in asking for changes, such as those highlighted in Table 34.

In truth, it is crucial that unions continue to be mobilized in order to ensure socially acceptable outcomes through collective bargaining. However, the achievement of social and economic protections for all workers is far from being certain (Blum 2008).

In: Private Equity Globalisation   ISBN: 978-1-53615-043-8
Editor: M. Madi   © 2019 Nova Science Publishers, Inc.

Chapter 6

PRIVATE EQUITY GLOBAL EXPANSION

6.1. RISKS IN PRIVATE EQUITY BUSINESS

Risk management in the private equity industry is different to public markets for several reasons (Diller and Jackel 2015). First, while the typical and well-known risk measures of public markets (price volatility, value-at-risk) are globally spread, there is no market price available on a regular basis to adequately measure the market risk for the PE asset class. Indeed, market fluctuations impact on the value of the investments held in the portfolio (assets/portfolio companies).[1] In short, market risk refers to the risk of holding an asset whose value changes over time.

Second, a private equity fund is used as the investment vehicle to search and select companies, manage them actively, define their strategies in order to create more value and sell them after an average holding period of five years. In this attempt, investors can run a liquidity risk. Private equity investors are also exposed to asset liquidity risk associated with the sale of the companies in the secondary market at a discount rate. Indeed, the secondary market is not an efficient liquid market since secondary market prices are not often significantly influenced by market fundamentals.

---

[1] According to Diller and Jackel (2015), the closest estimation of market risk might be Interim NAV volatility. However, this quarterly valuations only covers parts of the underlying risk that may not reflect the real underlying value of the assets.

Third, investors also run funding risks as they might lose the capital already paid into the fund if they are not able to pay any further capital call required by previous agreement. Moreover, each investor can be negatively impacted as a result of other investors defaulting. Uncertainties about cash flows pose funding risks to investors since defaulting on payments results in the loss of private equity partnership interests. This risk is also referred to as default risk. Funding risks are relevant, mainly when a market instability or financial turmoil foster a mismatch of capital calls and distributions for investors. Moreover, after an equity market downturn, M&A deals might be closed at low market prices. However, the risk of losing capital can be reduced even to close to zero for a portfolio of 50 funds, as multiple evidences show.

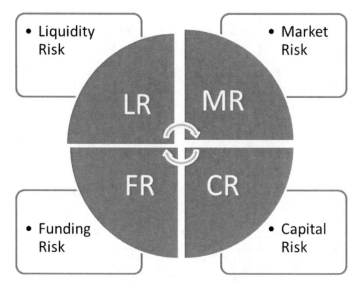

Source: adapted from Diller and Jackel (2015).

Figure 2. Private Equity Economic Risks.

Fourth, exit strategies can affect the capital risk by numerous factors, including management practices, leverage, interest rates, foreign exchange and macroeconomic scenario. Alike market risk, capital risk is influenced both by internal and external factors. First, in the long-term, the performance of the portfolio companies affects the capital risk of the PE investments. Positive operational and financial backgrounds, beyond market conditions, are sources of value creation during the holding periods. Second, the availability of debt and refinancing possibilities might influence long-term capital risk. Investors can manage their long-term risks through diversification in multiple PE funds with portfolio companies that belong to different regions, industries, stages of funding and holding periods. Moreover, co-investments and funds of funds might further increase the scope of those diversification strategies.

Moreover, it is well remembering that the risk dimensions of business models also depend on social, cultural and political values such as equity control, trust and transparency.

6.2. LARGEST PRIVATE EQUITY FUNDS

The ranking below shows the largest five private equity firms in 2008 and 2017. Ten years after the global crisis, the private equity firm Carlyle still remains at the top. Today, on terms of aggregate capital raised, it is followed by the Blackstone Group, KKR, Goldman Sachs and Ardian (Table 35).

According Preqin (2017) Global Private Equity & Venture Capital Report, the PE industry has presented a trend towards greater concentration of total assets under management with the largest funds accounting for a greater proportion of overall fundraising. With the greater capital concentration seen in recent years, the average size of private equity funds has grown from US$384million in 2016 to US$535million in 2017. In addition to the growing levels of capital raised, there has been a trend to huge capital overhang or dry powder, that is to say, accumulated capital that is still searching for profitable deals. Table 36 shows the largest ten private equity firms in addition to the amounts of capital raised and to the levels of capital overhang accumulated in the period between 2007 and 2016.

Even though fewer funds closed in 2017 (921 funds) than in 2016 (1,243 funds), there has not been observed increasing fundraising or liquidity risks

94 *Maria Alejandra Madi*

as market conditions have improved. Table 37 shows the size, type and geographic focus of the largest 10 private equity funds closed in the second quarter of 2018.

Table 35. Private equity firms: The biggest five in the world, 2008 and 2017

Rank	Year	PE firm	Capital raised
1	2008	Carlyle Group	US$52 billion aggregate capital raised in the last 5 years
	2017	Carlyle Group	US$66.7 billion aggregate capital raised in the last 10 years
2	2008	Goldman Sachs	US$49.05 billion aggregate capital raised in the last 5 years
	2017	Blackstone Group	US$62.2 billion aggregate capital raised in the last 10 years
3	2008	TPG Fort Worth	US$48.75 billion aggregate capital raised in the last 5 years
	2017	KKR	US$59.7 billion aggregate capital raised in the last 10 years.
4	2008	Kohlberg Kravis Roberts	US$39.67 billion aggregate capital raised in the last 5 years
	2017	Goldman Sachs	US$55.6 billion aggregate capital raised in the last 10 years
5	2008	CVC Capital Partners	US$36.84 billion aggregate capital raised in the last 5 years
	2017	Ardian	US$53.4 billion aggregate capital raised in the last 10 years

Source: Elaborated by the author. Adapted from IUF (2008a) and Preqin (2017).
Note: May 2008 and April 2017.

Table 36. Largest private equity firms: Capital raised and capital overhang, 2007 and 2016, US$billion

Rank	PE firm	Headquarter	Capital raised	Capital overhang
1	Carlyle Group	US	66,7	15,8
2	Blackstone Group	US	62,2	31,9
3	KKR	US	57,9	17,6
4	Goldman Sachs	US	55,6	16,0
5	Ardian	France	53,4	22,3
6	TPG	US	47,0	12,9
7	CVC Capital Partners	UK	42,2	10,6
8	Warburg Pincus	US	41,6	12,9
9	Advent International	US	40,9	14,4
10	Bain Capital	US	37,7	10,0

Source: Preqin (2017b).

Table 37. Largest private equity funds closed in Q2 2018

Rank	PE fund	PE firm	Geographic focus	Fund Size, in mn	Fund Type
1	Carlyle Asia Partners V	Carlyle Group	Asia	6,550 USD	Buyout
2	Bain Capital Europe V	Bain Capital	Europe	4,350 EUR	Buyout
3	Nordic Capital Fund DC	Nordic Capital	Europe	4,300 EUR	Buyout
4	TowerBrook Investors V	TowerBrook Capital Partners	US	4,250 USD	Buyout
5	General Atlantic Investment Partners 2017	General Atlantic	US	3,289 EUR	Buyout

Table 37. (Continued)

Rank	PE fund	PE firm	Geographic focus	Fund Size, in mn	Fund Type
6	Thomas Bravo Discover Fund II	Thomas Bravo	US	2,400 USD	Buyout
7	Blackstone Capital Partners Asia	Blackstone Group	Asia	2,300 USD	Buyout
8	BGH Capital Fund I	BGH Capital	Australasia	2,600 AUD	Buyout
9	Inflexion Buyout Fund V	Inflexion Private Equity Partners	Europe	1,250 GBP	Buyout
10	Atlas Capital Resources III	Atlas Holdings	US	1,675 USD	Buyout

Source: Preqin (2018).

6.3. GEOGRAPHIC FOCUS: DIVERSIFICATION STRATEGIES

Nowadays, the US is still home to the greatest number of top private equity funds, followed by West Europe and then China. According to Bloomberg, the 5 major countries in global private equity deal volume have been: United States (55%), Britain (10%), China (8%), Australia (4%) and Germany (2.4%).[2] Taking into account risk management strategies, diversification is a relevant tool to reduce risk in the industry. According to Preqin (2017a) survey with investors, 69% of investors surveyed believe in North America best opportunities, while nearly a third of respondents believe Asia is increasing in importance. Taking into account the volume of fundraising at January 2018, North America continues to dominate with 50% of the number of funds and 45% of the total capital raised. However, Asia-focused funds represent seven of the 10 largest funds that correspond to over a third of total capital raised. Outside North America, Europe and Asia, private equity funds faced a particularly tough year in 2017: 56% of total

---

[2] For more details see Heberlein (2018). https://www.toptal.com/finance/private-equity-consultants/private-equity-industry.

capital was raised by GPs based in Africa, Latin America, the Middle East, Israel and Australasia. Over half of funds closed in 2017 were of the venture capital type, followed by growth (23%) and buyout (14%). Table 38 outlines findings about the geographic focus of the private equity industry, as of January 2018.

6.3.1. Traditional Private Equity Markets: North America and Europe

According to Preqin (2018), capital concentration has been more prominent in North America than in any other region in 2017. Among other relevant market features, mega fund closures led the fundraising scenario, such as Apollo Global Management's (Apollo Investment Fund IX) that has been considered the largest PE fund ever fundraised. Within global markets, in the period prior to 2016, venture capital deals had been increasing for six consecutive years. On 2015, the record was of 13,019 deals. After 2016, there has been a trend of fewer but higher valued deals. In North America, almost 50% of the funds closed in 2017 were venture capital funds.

Table 38. Private equity funds: Geographic focus, January 2018

	Number of Funds Raising	Aggregate Capital Targeted (US$billion)
North America	1,152	338
Europe	372	99
Asia	509	266
Rest of the World	263	41

Source: Preqin Equity Online.

According to the Bain & Company (2018b) report on Asia-Pacific, in recent years, there has been a movement away from North America, shifting towards Europe and emerging opportunities in Greater China. As of 2017:

- The deal flow in North America reached its lowest level since 2010. As a result, the region's market share (39%) was lower than its 58% historical average (2007-2016).

- Greater China presented more deals and its market share amounted 24%, above the 11% average in 2007-2016.
- The European PE deals were at its lowest level since 2012, although its market share of 19% decreased only 1% of its historical average in 2007-2016.

In Europe, total fundraising in 2017 was a record since 2006. The main investors were: pension funds (29%), funds of funds (20%), family offices & private individuals (15%), sovereign wealth funds (9%) and insurance companies (8%). Non-European institutional investors invested more than 40%, mainly investors from Asia with a 15% share. Looking at the levels of fundraising by the type of private equity funds, buyout funds were followed by the venture capital ones.

According to Preqin, European-focused fundraising had a strong year in 2017 where private equity buyouts accounted for 73% of total capital rose, followed by secondary funds (10%) and venture capital funds (7%). Western Europe-focused funds increased the amount of capital raised in 2016 with an average bigger initial target size. In this scenario, UK-based private equity firms continued to dominate fundraising, securing 53% of the capital raised. Moreover, it is worth noting that the UK private equity market continues to be relevant despite Brexit uncertainties.

Indeed, the total amount invested in European companies increased between 2016 and 2017. Ten years after the 2008 global crisis, mega buyouts represented nearly 40% of the buyout market, while venture capital investment increased by 34% and surpassed 2008's amount. Among the 5 most relevant economic sectors that received the highest amount of investments, we can highlight consumer goods & services, business products & services, ICT (communication, computer and electronics), biotech & healthcare, and financial & insurance activities. The economic sectors that received the lowest amount of investments were agriculture, real state, energy & environment, transportation, construction and chemicals & materials.

After the strong exit years of 2014 and 2015, the year of 2017 was also relevant for exit strategies, mainly trade sale (35%), sale to another private equity firm (28%) and IPO (14%). Buyout exits amounted 76% of all exits in value and 23% by number of companies, most exits belong to business products & services, followed by consumer goods & services, communication, computer & electronics, biotech & healthcare, and financial & insurance activities. The economic sectors that presented the lowest amount of exits were agriculture, real state, transportation, energy & environment, chemicals & materials and construction. As of 2018, changes in the private equity industry continued to foster the expansion of megafunds.

6.3.2. The Shift to the Asia-Pacific Region

China turned out to be the most attractive emerging market private equity destination, followed by India. Ten years after the global crisis, the Asia-Pacific region can be considered as a relevant target for deal making. Taking into account the Asia-Pacific region, PE funds are generally classified on behalf of their location and the profile of investors: i) Pure offshore non-RMB funds set up outside of China with foreign investors, ii) Foreign invested RMB funds located in China with Chine investors and at least one foreign investor, iii) Pure domestic RMB funds located in China without foreign investors (Deloitte 2013).

According to Preqin (2018), the concentration trend, already observed both in the US and Europe, has recently been noted in Asia. While Asia-based GPs invested 78% of capital on the region, China and India remained relevant for vehicles that enhanced venture capital deals. Table 39 presents a sample of the Asia-Pacific PE deals in 2017.

Ten year after the 2008 global crisis, Asia-Pacific-focused funds held 23% of global private equity assets under management, a record from the market share of 9% a decade ago. The number of Asia-Pacific funds amounted 194 in 2017, with average size of US$ 340 milion, while in the period 2012-2016, the average number was 325, with average size of US$190m. A key driver of the concentration trend was the expansion of consortium transactions that enhanced megadeals over $1 billion, including the region's largest buyout ever—the $14.7 billion acquisition of Toshiba's semiconductor business by Bain Capital and others. In this scenario, public-to-private deals amounted 17% of total Asia-Pacific deal value and the multiples remain higher than the current US average of 10.3. The total value of the region's PE deals increased to 17% of Asia-Pacific mergers & acquisitions transactions, while public-to-private deals more than doubled.

Greater China (China, Hong Kong and Taiwan) has been attracting the most capital in 2017 while Japan and Southeast Asia gained market share in fundraising. The LPs' interest in the region has fostered the levels of dry powder to 2.2 years of future supply at the current pace of 2017 investment, also in venture capital and growth private equity funds. Table 40 shows other relevant findings about the investment scenario.

Table 39. Asia-Pacific private equity firms: Deals by type and focus, 2017

PE firm	Fund type	Focus
KKR	Buyout	Regional
CITIC Private Equity	Multi-estrategy	China
Asia Alternatives Management	Fund of Funds	Regional
Baidu	Expansion/large stage	China
Quadrant Private Equity	Buyout	Australia/New Zealand

Source: Bain & Company (2018b).

Indeed, nowadays China ranks as the world's second-largest venture capital market behind Silicon Valley. And also India has been expanding the market in terms of venture capital and growth private equity deals. From 2014 to September 2017, LPs received US$1.20 for every US$1 invested. Comparing private and public companies, buyout and growth funds performance almost doubled the returns of public companies in a perspective of three, ten or twenty years.

Higher valuations are also part of the investment trends. The internet and technology sectors attracted 46% of the deal volume in 2017, while this participation in total deals was of 22% in 2012. Some recent examples include SoftBank Capital's investment in Flipkart Online Services in India, or the Singapore-based Grab deal led by a consortium of investors including Toyota's Next Technology Fund and SoftBank Capital. LPs also continued to focus on consumption-related sectors, including consumer products, retail and healthcare.

Table 40. Asia-Pacific private equity: Investment data, 2012-2017

Period	PE Investment Value		Deal Count		Average deal (US$m)	
	2012-2016 average	2017	2012-2016 average	2017	2012-2016 average	2017
Greater China	47	73	444	569	105	128
Japan	7	25	48	69	141	504
Southeast Asia	7	20	62	70	114	284
India	13	20	221	184	58	106
South Korea	10	13	77	91	126	140
Australia/New Zealand	9	9	47	51	184	175

Source: Bain & Company (2018).

As GPs have searched to gain more control over the portfolio companies in the Asia-Pacific region, buyouts represented 45% of deal value in 2017. There was also an increase in minority deals that include board seats, decision rights and path-to-control provisions. Indeed, the fact that company owners are more willing to cede control might enhance the expansion of the Asia-Pacific private equity industry.

Within this region, private equity investments have been more balanced geographically. Despite the relevant role of Greater China that accounted 45% of the region's PE activity, India, Japan and Southeast Asia each represented more than 10% of total deal value. In short, two key forces powered growth in 2017: investors' growing confidence in the region, and company owners' greater overall acceptance of PE funding.

Moreover, exit strategies have been successful, particularly in countries like India, where the PE industry has historically faced challenges to generate good returns. The average net internal rate of return (IRR) was 11.5% as of January 2018. According the Bain & Company 2018 Asia-Pacific Private Equity survey, the value and number of exits (710) rose in all countries across the region, with particularly strong rebounds in Southeast Asia and South Korea. Among the trade exits, Anchorage, Oaktree, TPG and York Capital led the divestment of Alinta Energy (Australia); Bain Capital, Goldman Sachs and Lee Song-ok led the exit of Carver Korea (South Korea) and Goldman Sachs, MBK, PAG and Owl Creek led the exit of Universal Studios Japan (Japan). Singapore's sovereign wealth fund, GIC, led the largest exit that included trade and secondary exit channels. In this setting, secondary sales also increased and IPOs followed the historical average.

Despite the recent success, the near-future Asia-Pacific region competitive challenges are: regional/local private equity firms, global corporate players, global PE funds, investment strategies of LPs, cross-border private equity investments. Table 41 outlines key features of the performance and market outlook.

Selected information from Table 41 suggests that higher deal values will be a probable trend in the Asia-Pacific region. In this scenario, the creation of value and competitive advantages in the portfolio companies will increasingly rely on:

- Building commercial excellence, including customer segmentation, product offerings, pricing and sale channels.
- Improving management skill and adopting digital technologies, including market data strategies, Big Data, analytics and connectivity.

Despite the relevance of digital strategies, the Bain & Company 2018 report on the Asia-Pacific region highlights that less than 5% of GPs believe that are fully prepared to manage digital disruption and almost 60% say that they do not have the relevant digital tools to diagnose a company's competitive strengths or weaknesses over the next three to five years.

BOX: ASIA-PACIFIC CASE STUDIES

Courts Asia

In 2007, when the PE fund Baring Private Equity Asia acquired a majority stake in Courts Asia, it was a traditional retailer with very low performance, an overextended store network and poor customer research data that sold few products online. In 2010, Courts and the private equity firm Baring started a broader transformation. The first step was the restructuring of the store network, cost reduction and improvement of commercial strategies. As soon as the performance started to improve, an accelerating growth program focused on multiple channel retailing in Southeast Asia was launched. Moreover, touch points gather continual feedback from customers. As of 2012, the IPO was successful because of the leading role of Courts Asia in the Asian Market. In the exist transaction, the value of Baring's stake more than doubled. By 2014, Courts led traditional home and electronics retailers in Asia.

Qingdao Haier

In 2013, the private equity firm KKR acquired a 10% stake in China's Qingdao Haier, a global household electrical appliances company, and became its strategic partner. Up to 2013, Haier has been growing slowly but had a shrinking market share. Despite the focus on the creation of a digital business model had started before the KKK deal, after the acquisition, KKR and Haier worked closely to develop a strategy that used Big Data and artificial intelligence to improve the interaction with customers, to understand their needs and preferences (prices, security or leisure opportunities). The aim is to offer the right categories of products and services and to use Big Data and artificial intelligence to optimize products and improve customers' experience. Ultimately, the digital strategy helped Haier to be resilient and to adapt the business model to a fast-changing market. Four years after the deal, the value of the exit deal revealed that Haier's stock price had almost tripled.

Carver Korea

After the private equity deal, Carver Korea, a leading Korean cosmetics brand, redefined the growth strategy to transform the business model. Four key drivers improve the performance: i) customer segmentation with the expansion of a new on line segment oriented to young people, ii) improvement of the consistency of the "Aesthetic" brand identity, iii) simplification of product lines and elimination of underperforming product models, iv) redefinition of delivery channels by expanding online, besides the expansion in drugstores, duty-free shops and exports to China. The major organizational change was the shift from the founder organization to expert teams. As a result, Carver Korea tripled its annual growth from 2012 to 2015 before selling a 60% stake to Bain Capital and Goldman Sachs in 2016.

Source: Bain & Company (2018b).

**Table 41. Asia-Pacific private equity Funds:
Performance and market outlook, 2017**

Period	2017 performance		Near future PE market outlook	
	Deals	Sectors	Investment flows	Competition
Greater China	Record of deal value, led by megadeals and buyouts. Active exit transactions.	Internet, logistics, consumer and services.	Buyout and path to control. Dry powder.	Growing competition.
India	Lower deal activity with a few megadeals. Active exit transactions.	Internet and technology.	More balanced sector focus. Improvements in exit channels.	High valuation and competition. Concerns about LPs investing directly.
Japan	High record of deals. Active trade exits.	Technology.	Non-core diversification strategies. Larger transactions. More trust of company owners.	Increasing competition.
Australia	Deals aligned with historical average. Challenges for IPOs as exit channel.	Healthcare.	High expertise and fundraising availability.	Concerns about LPs investing directly. High deal value.
South Korea	Active deal activity and secondary exits.	Consumer, retail, energy and natural resources.	Strong flows.	Higher deal valuations and competition.

Source: Elaborated by the author. Adapted from Bain & Company (2018).

Today, most private equity firms are still developing leadership-assessment capabilities to assess the management team during due diligence or after the acquisition. Indeed, organization challenges have been pointed out as key drivers of exits failures, such as lack of managerial skills, lack of focus on wrong issues, bad-dimensioned plans, lack of alignments between GPs and portfolio companies. Among the drivers of success, we can highlight: top-managers´s skills, alignment between GPs and portfolio companies, reduced costs and successful margin growth.

6.4. PRIVATE EQUITY REGULATION

The 2008 global financial crisis created new demands for reform and regulation since financialisation of the economies fostered higher leverage and risk-taking. Looking back, after the 1960s, the US government has gradually loosened restrictions on the commercial banking system. This process culminated in the late 1990s with the end of the Glass-Stegall Act of 1933 that had prevented commercial banks from acting as investment banks for decades. This trend was followed by most Western countries.

Table 42. Private equity regulation: Literature review

Research results	References
Within the segments of the M&A market, those dominated by PE firms are among the most competitive of all. In this sense, antitrust allegations are not usual.	Comment, Robert. 2013. "Team Bidding by Private Equity Sponsors: Are the Antitrust Allegations Plausible?" *Journal of Applied Finance* 23 (1).
The relation between PE managers and investors still requires broader monitoring and regulations by policymakers.	Morris, Peter and Phalippou, Ludovic. 2011."A New Approach to Regulating Private Equity" *The Journal of Corporate Law Studies* 12 (1): 59-84.
Despite the regulatory regime after 2008, hedge and PE funds are not well differentiated in the European regulatory framework "Alternative Investment Fund Managers Directive" (AIFMD)	Payne, Jennifer. 2011. "Private Equity and its Regulation in Europe." *Oxford Legal Studies* Research Paper No. 40.

Source: Elaborated by the author. Adapted from BVCA Research Academic Portal. https://www.bvca.co.uk/Research/Academic-Research-Portal.

Among the lessons learned, the 2008 global crisis showed that financial regulation can foster the adoption of better practices but cannot eliminate the emergence of crisis. Indeed, there is a delay between regulation patterns and practices that favor financial innovations. Another challenge to financial stability is the growth of the shadow banking system that ranges from non-banks, such as private equity firms, money market mutual funds and hedge funds.

Table 42 sheds light on the PE regulatory framework, mainly on the research evidences on transparency, disclosure and systemic risks that, so far, have been among the main concerns.

Considering the PE industry, the amount of regulation has been increasing in recent years. In the period from 2013-2018 several tax proposals have been agreed at the European Union level and the priorities have been transparency and disclosure of tax information[3] - including financial account information, cross-border tax rulings, country-by-country reporting, access to certain anti-money laundering data and requirements on intermediaries to disclose tax planning schemes with a cross-border element. The Alternative Investment Fund Managers Directive (AIFMD or Directive 2011/61/EU) is the main European regulation measure that affects the operation, reporting and marketing of private equity and venture capital funds. After being adopted by the European Union in July 2011, it took effect on 22 July 2013. This Directive created a pan-European regulatory framework for Alternative Investment Fund Managers (AIFMs), including private equity, venture capital, real estate and hedge funds, among others. Fully authorised AIFMs received an EEA passport to market and manage EU AIFs in third countries. This fact is relevant in light of Brexit. Moreover, the European Venture Capital Fund Regulation (EuVECA) is a voluntary regime that introduces a marketing passport regime for venture capital fund managers. The adoption of the EuVECA by the VC sector has been slow, mainly because of the restrictive eligibility criteria for the size of company funds. EuVECA is currently under review by the European Commission to include slight improvements oriented toto liberalise the eligibility criteria and reduce administrative costs.

In 2016, the Anti-Tax Avoidance Directive was agreed upon by Member States in order to introduce rules on interest deductibility, exit taxation, a general anti-abuse provision, controlled foreign companies, and hybrid mismatches. Indeed, the movement in the field of taxation has grown

---

[3] For further details, see Invest Europe and KPMG (2018). htps://www.investeurope.eu/media/722513/IE_Tax-Benchmark-Study-2018.pdf.

recently, such as the publication of the draft bill of law regarding the transposition of the first Anti-Tax Avoidance Directive into national legislation in 2018. Other regulatory and market developments - the Common Reporting Standard (CRS), the Market Financial Instruments Directive (MiFID II) and the OECD/G20 BEPS Project on international tax rules (BEPS) - have put great pressure on the private equity agenda. GPs have reacted rapidly by implementing deep changes varying from reviewing the existing corporate structure, operating model and internal controls (LPEA 2018).[4]

Taking into account the US regulation, the SEC mandated that buyout firms should comply with the 2010 Dodd-Frank Act as of June 2011. Therefore, the regulator has legal recourse to audit buyout firms' financials in detail. After that, the SEC's Office of Compliance Inspections and Examination discovered illegal fees and compliance shortfalls in more than half of the 112 buyout firms investigated. In the SEC 2014 report titled *Spreading Sunshine in Private Equity*, GPs' reports are accused to enhance opacity in information related to potential problems in portfolio companies. Another area of controversy for regulators has been the income tax rate on fund managers' fees. As a result of the "Carried Interest Fairness Act of 2015" bill, the US government could be raising as much as US$180 billion over ten years. With more countries following the leading examples of the US and European Union, regulation is a topic that will continue to add complexity to the day to day operation of private equity funds. In 2017, the SEC has increasingly monitored GPs on behalf of the inaccurate disclosure of private equity fees and the new reporting guidelines from the Institutional Limited Partners Association (ILPA) over credit lines in order to foster greater transparency (Preqin 2018).

---

[4] In this setting of changes in competition and regulation, the decision about Brexit could turn out to favour Luxembourg as a primary location in Europe (LPEA 2018). As a matter of fact: i)Luxembourg is reinforcing its leading position as an alternative fund location, and ii) despite regulations that provoke administrative burdens across Europe, Luxembourg continues to enjoy a stable political and tax environment that it is now welcoming small and medium size players

PART III: PRIVATE EQUITY EXPANSION AND THE "NEW NORMAL"

In: Private Equity Globalisation   ISBN: 978-1-53615-043-8
Editor: M. Madi   © 2019 Nova Science Publishers, Inc.

Chapter 7

PRIVATE EQUITY TODAY AND TOMORROW

7.1. THE NEW NORMAL

After the 1970s, the reorganization of the markets at the global level has been overwhelmed by the financial logic of investment in a setting characterized by expansion of credit, capital markets' operations and institutional investors (Crotty 2002). Within this framework, Professor Lazonick's research highlights the impacts of the shift to the value extraction criteria under a "downsize-and-distribute" corporate governance regime, legitimated in the name of shareholder-value maximization. As a matter of fact, corporations' strategies turned out to be focused on short-term gains and the distribution of dividends to shareholders, that is to say, to investors (Lazonick and Sullivan 2000). In this global scenario context, PE funds became a driver of globalisation.

From an economics point of view, these trends suggest new questions because of their implications on market competition and financial instability. The global network of interactions between power-holders require a new systemic approach to financial instability in contemporary capitalism since companies have potentially wide and indirect influence on the evolution of the levels of investment, production and employment at the local levels. Indeed, the density of the interconnections between the financial and non-financial companies in a network might increase global systemic risks. As the interest of private companies does not generally coincide with the interests of society as a whole, these risks need to be dealt with new anti-trust practices and new rules on cross-ownerships among corporations.

No more than ever, people in Europe, Asia, Africa, North and South America are sharing either prosperity or destitution. The tensions and challenges of these troubled times do not only affect policy makers, but also the academic discourse. The realities of globalisation show that there is a new rationale for spreading not only economic (fiscal) discipline as well as political repression. In fact, new rationale, that also supports the war on drugs and on terrorism, has been already on the drawing board.

According to James Galbraith (2015), placing the outcomes of the 2008 global crisis in the long-term, we are living under " the end of normal" since the challenges for actual output growth have become deeper. Among those challenges, Galbraith highlights:

- "Secular stagnation" has lowered the level of potential output and dampened potential growth.
- The nature of technical change seems to negatively affect output growth and employment levels since it is labour-saving.
- Energy markets remain both high cost and uncertain.
- The private financial sector has ceased to be a driver of growth.
- The world order is no longer under the effective financial and military control of the United States and its allies.

In this scenario, the private equity industry has displayed resilience in a time characterized by slow global growth. The term resilience has been reframed in terms of flexible adaptation in a scenario characterised by turbulent and unpredictable economic dynamics. Indeed, resilience is also at stake in the context of the PE funds' recent performance. In this scenario, the main questions to be addressed are: *How is the private equity business model engaging in a "new normal" scenario? How are General Partners (GPs) adjusting to this "new normal" of high cost deals and high competition?*

Indeed, General Partners are getting more proactive in the search of strategies to achieve higher growth and returns, as outlined in Table 43.

Table 43. The new normal: Private equity management strategies, 2017

Strategy	Objectives
Active portfolio management	Searching promising companies, also within portfolios of other PE funds that might be for sale. Among the promising companies in terms of profitability, GPs aim at increasing the levels of patient capital, that is to say, investments in founder-led businesses that need capital to grow.
Risk management	The objective is to build stronger capabilities to address risk management and face the new challenges in the good and services markets.
Public-to-private buyouts	Looking for promising deals where GPs can take public companies private since there are available lenders for these bigger transactions.
Expansion through add-ons	The objective is to add smaller firms to the PE portfolio because they can be acquired at lower prices.
Long-term perspective in fund-raising and investment	The objective is to adopt new strategies while extending the holding period of the portfolio investments in order to increase the value creation before the exit. So far, there are different types of long-hold PE funds, such as: • buyout funds that favor lower risk/ return in portfolio companies and search for stable and low-growth assets; • buyout funds that target risk and return profiles in line with the traditional ones.
Lower transaction costs	The objective is to improve tax planning through, for instance, deferred taxation of capital gains to allow capital to compound over time. Besides, the reduction of taxes and consultant fees are being considered.
Acquisition of sufficient large stakes in companies	The objective is to gain board representation and decision rights to influence the PE portfolio compositon, the investment flows and the profit targets.
Other efficiency strategies	The objective is to enhance complementary investments in the set of portfolio companies.

Source: Elaborated by the author. Adapted from Bain (2015 and 2018).

Table 43 shows how are GPs responding to the current situation through turning to a mix of strategies. To compete with corporate buyers in M&A, especially for large assets, LPs and GPs need to take decisions in a "new normal" setting and behave more like corporations in order to extend the duration of their investments. Table 44 sheds light on some evidences of the recent shift from cost-reduction to organic growth.

Table 44. Private equity: Management practices, 2017

Strategy	Practices
Active portfolio management	This practice has been growing in Europe and other regions where GPs have been active in searching for lists of promising candidates for new deals.
Risk management	On behalf of new consumption trends, KKR's carve-out of Unilever's spreads business needs to face the challenge of declining consumption of margarine.
Public-to-private buyouts	This practice has been relevant and the total value of deals almost doubled the level of 2016 and jumped to US$180 billion in 2017.
Expansion through add-ons	In the retail health sector, more firms, especially in North America, are adopting this practice.
Long-term perspective in fund-raising and investment	Some examples can be highlighted: • Blackstone raised US$5 billion for a buyout with a target holding period of almost 10 years. • Core Equity and Cove Hill raised more than US$1 billion each with a target holding period of up to 15 years. • CVC raised capital for a buyout fund with an investment holding period of 15-years. • Cranemere Group raised capital for funds where investors become shareholders with controlling governance rights.
Lower transaction costs	GPs need to disclosure new regulations, such as the American regulation that has issued guidance related to takeovers where debt exceeds 6 times the EBITDA.

Source: Elaborated by the author. Adapted from Bain (2015 and 2018).

Nowadays, the PE business model cannot be only committed to old habits. Indeed, GPs have historically relied on cost-cutting strategies and market conditions to achieve the targets. Today's new technologies transform commercial capabilities (Big Data, CRM data, and social media activity). Focusing on cost reduction and underestimating a company's exposure to technological disruption is certainly a wrong strategy.

In the current business scenario, rebuilding strategies also require the modernization of commercial capabilities and a new management profile. In the new management scenario, GPs should focus:

- On the activities of the portfolio companies in terms of customer and delivery channels, operations, products and services.
- How the PE portfolio company delivers the goods & services, considering digital platforms and partners, data and analytics, IT, operating models, suppliers and workers.

What is at stake is the ability of GPs to enhance profitable organic growth that requires a kind of management that aims at facing the firms' vulnerabilities in their specific markets in a scenario where the digital economy is transforming how companies identify, understand and serve their customers. According to the Ernst & Young (2016) Private Equity Survey, PE funds have started to invest in new software for portfolio analytics and management, digital platforms supporting better communication with investors, and increased automation of routine processes. As a result, exit transactions might be different from traditional ones in the next future. After 2010, the average global buyout holding period has been up to five years. In the near future, longer holding periods will likely be the "new normal".

7.2. THE DIGITIZATION OF BUSINESS

At the beginning of XX century, Joseph Schumpeter developed the concept of *creative destruction* to characterize the waves of development based on clusters of innovations -both technical and institutional. In the last decades, these waves have included petrochemical products, automobiles, information technologies and biotechnologies, especially genetic modification.

Looking back, throughout the postwar era in advanced Western societies, scientific research and technological development included research councils, scientific advisory boards, expert commissions and specialized government agencies in different areas, such as health, agriculture and atomic energy. The target was to transform the scientific and technological development in a profitable process. For instance, new kinds of chemical products have been introduced mainly fertilizers, insecticides and additives used in food production.

The historical changes in business have been related to qualitative transformations in capital accumulation and competition. Public policies and private strategies influenced the dimension and composition of balance sheets in different economic sectors. Among the new features:

- The household sector has got increasingly indebted.
- Corporations have moved to "surplus units" running financial surpluses that have been diverted towards the acquisition of financial assets instead of financing physical investments.
- The balance sheets of investment funds are now larger than ever before and they influence investment flows.
- The changing practices in corporate finance fostered the growth of institutional investors, such as PE funds, in business management as relevant shareholders that fostered the market of mergers & acquisitions.

Looking at the evolution of the global business models since the 2000s, the strategies of private equity funds have turned out to focus on short-term gains. In other words, the current PE business model can be apprehended as a form of governance that aims increasing short-term earnings by means of a "clash of rationalization". Accordingly the OECD, the current investment chain is complex due to complex interactions between investors and managers. In this scenario, the economic and social outcomes have involved a trend to 'downsize and distribute', that is to say, a trend to restructure, reduce costs and focus on short- term gains. In practice this has meant plants displacement and closures, changed in working conditions, outsourcing and pressure on global supply chain producers. Within current business strategies, investments that are fixed for society turn out to be liquid for investors. Today, the dominance of a culture based on short-termism has major implications that go far beyond the narrow confines of the financial markets. The costs of this business model fall disproportionately on society because of the commitment to *liquidity*.

How Competitiveness and Productivity Have Been Put Together in the Attempt to Promote Higher Private Equity Performance?

Technology transforms the business scenario as the result of the diffusion of new practices at the micro-level. According to Jeremy Rifkin, the technological structure will create multiple connections to companies, governments, buildings via sensors and software to the Internet of Things platform that will feed Big Data in real time. Many leading global Information Technology companies are already working on the build-out of the Internet of Things infrastructure for a Third Industrial Revolution. Among the initiatives, we can highlight GE's "Industrial Internet", Cisco's "Internet of Things", IBM's "Smarter Planet" and Siemen's "Sustainable Cities" that use advanced analytics to analyse Big Data and create predictive algorithms into automated systems. Accordingly Rifkin, this process will improve efficiencies, increase productivity, and reduce the marginal cost of producing and delivering a full range of goods and services across the entire economy. In an increasingly automated world, workers are being polarized into high-tech works and a growing number of displaced workers who have few prospects for meaningful job opportunities.

Accordingly Eric Hobsbawn (1995), deep concerns turned out to grow because of the social implications of these scientific and technological trends. Indeed, in Western societies, signals of social discontent included the critique of science and technology applied to military targets, and of the deleterious effects of automation technologies on labour and working conditions. In addition, high concern also arose on behalf of health and environmental costs of the widely-used chemical in agriculture. More recently, the outcomes of globalisation revealed the impacts of financial and business interests on scientific and technological development.

More recently, the digitization of the economy has fostered the transformation of traditional business models under Fordism. According to Aubourg and Coekelbergs (2018), most PE portfolio companies have often not really assessed the risk of digital gap. Indeed, GPs should rethink how technological change can affect performance by implementing a digital transformation strategy in the portfolio companies in order to transform organisations, reduce costs and optimise data usage. Indeed, private equity funds require new tools and lenses to understand how technology affects industries, consumer products companies, distributors, equipment manufacturers and many other businesses. Bain & Company 2018 report on private equity highlights that GPs are exploring how technological change can affect profits and include among current digital strategies:

- Networks of IT providers, advanced analytics vendors or digital partners, specific to each sector, that can provide a foundation of digital support for portfolio companies;
- Centers of excellence within the private equity fund that allow portfolio companies access to proven solutions or best practices in areas like digital marketing or social media;
- Connections to outside digital thinkers with expertise in technologies or industries of special importance to the private equity fund, who can provide perspective on digital trends and what they mean for the portfolio companies;
- Better communication with investors in order to explain major technology trends and how they affect various industries represented in the fund portfolio.

Indeed, private equity funds require new tools and lenses to understand how technology affects industries, as evidenced by the rapid ascent of Amazon and its impact on retailers, consumer products companies, distributors, equipment manufacturers and many other businesses.

Within the PE ecosystem, the digitization of the economies is not only affecting the future of the portfolio companies but also the process of fundraising (LPEA, 2018b). It is worth remembering that in the last ten years the increasing digitalization of financial transactions has also been also related to changes in financial competition. The expansion of the startups called fintechs, mainly since 2010, has revealed a new articulation between finance and technology. As a result of the advance of new non-bank competitors (fintechs), big banks have begun to establish collaborative partnerships with selected fintechs in order to produce new technological solutions in the areas of payment systems, insurance, financial consultancy and management and digital currencies. In this digital environment, new technologies – such as advanced analytics, blockchains, Big Data, robotics, artificial intelligence can be highlighted. And also new forms of encryption and biometrics have enabled the provision of innovations in financial products and services that could challenge current central banks' patterns of policy and regulation.

Initial Coin Offerings (ICOs) and crowdfunding have been considered alternative ways to fundraising that mainly target "high net worth" or "well informed" investors. Structuring a PE fund issuing tokens requires permissioned blockchains in order to limit and identify the main actors and transparent practices (Aubourg and Coekelbergs 2018). While comparing tokens with securities, there is the belief that tokens are safe and can be traded 24/7, besides offering traceability and greater transparency. In terms of liquidity concerns, tokens can also be an alternative for private equity funds with rather illiquid underlying assets. However, there is still uncertainty in a context where, for instance, EU regulators have adopted a rather passive approach with messages to caution firms and investors.

Indeed, since the year of 2017, interest in cryptocurrencies and related digital assets have been increasing in the private equity industry (Emirdag 2018). Crypto assets have also been thought as an alternative through the venture capital sector despite concerns about anonymity, price volatility, liquidity and transparency. The expansion of the emerging cryptoasset class includes:

- Development of administration services for PE funds.
- Building models for the valuation of these alternative assets.
- Creation of custody services for cryptoassets.

- Creation of data services regarding cryptoassets.
- Regulatory frameworks to enhance a well-connected market structure.
- Development of new instruments to operate digital networks.

Traditional PE firms, such as Blackstone and Carlyle, are showing their ability to embrace the digital change. In September 2015, Carlyle acquired the British PA Consulting that is specialized in technology, innovation and public sector work. In July 2016, Blackstone added Jim Breyer- former investor in venture capital- to its board of directors. In February 2017, Blackstone acquired Aon Technology - the largest benefits administration platform in the US and a leading provider for cloud-based HR management systems. Among other things, GPs are integrating analytics and big data tools, among other innovations, to build digital marketing effective strategies and multiple delivery channels (McKinsey 2018).

In short, the creation of a digital ecosystem might include the following elements:

- A network of IT providers, advanced analytics vendors or digital partners, sector by sector, to be a resource of digital support for portfolio companies.
- Centers of excellence within the PE firms that give to the portfolio companies access to proven solutions or best practices in areas like digital marketing or social media.
- Connections to outside thinkers with expertise in technologies or industries with special importance to the PE firm. This pool could provide perspectives on digital trends and what they mean for the portfolio companies.
- An internal team to manage the ecosystem and oversee initiatives for the entire portfolio.

Indeed, today, digital innovations foster new opportunities for redesigning the private equity business model.

7.3. PRIVATE EQUITY, CLIMATE CHANGE AND ENERGY INVESTMENTS

Global warming and global CO2 emissions are interconnected. In 2018, heatwaves were observed in Europe, Asia, North America and northern Africa, while the extent of Arctic sea ice has been continuously dropping. The World Meteorological Organization (WMO) pointed out that the last four years (2015-2018) have been the warmest years on record. In particular, between January and October 2018, global average temperature increased 0.98 degrees Celsius above the levels of 1850-1900. If this trend continues, temperatures may rise by 3-5 degrees Celsius by 2100.

Global CO2 emissions have also been increasing. China and the US together account for more than 40% of the global total CO2 emissions, according to 2017 data from the European Commission's Joint Research Centre and the PBL Netherlands Environmental Assessment Agency. After the withdrawal from the Paris climate change agreement, the US's environmental policy shifted to a pro-fossil fuels agenda to overcome the disadvantage of American businesses and workers. Trump called climate change a "very, very expensive form of tax". Fossil fuel lobbies in Saudi Arabia, Russia and Canada are powerful forces against government climate policies. Moreover, it can be highlighted that Australia is still dependent on coal exports.

In this global setting, the rise in investments in coal reveals the complex challenges and possibilities of effective global agreements. The scenario of the COP 24 certainly reveals these tensions. The 2018 Conference of the Parties (COP) in Katowice has been announced as the most critical since the 2015 Paris Agreement. In 2017, global emissions were 53.5 billion tons of carbon dioxide while the promises made in 2015 amounted 53 billion tons up to 2030.

The 2018 United Nations report warned that, in 2030, global greenhouse gas emissions could be between 13 billion and 15 billion tons higher than the level required keeping global warming within 2 degrees Celsius. Indeed, policy makers are currently at pressure to make progress since the Intergovernmental Panel on Climate Change (IPCC) 2018 report also highlighted that it is urgent to limit the global temperature increase to 1.5 degrees Celsius. In this attempt, governments should have to reduce emissions of greenhouse gases by around 25 percent and 55 percent lower than 2017 to limit global warming to 2 degrees and 1.5 degrees Celsius respectively.

Regarding this background, climate finance can be a tool to accelerate effective de-carbonization of the economy by means of: progress on energy efficiency, decarbonisation, electrification carbon capture and storage, afforestation and reforestation. Overall, global and local investments in electricity continue to fall far short of what is needed to close the energy access gap. In Africa and Asia, while international private finance more than doubled from the 2013-14 level to amount USD 2.9 billion in 2015-16, international public finance declined from USD 10.5 billion in 2013-14 to USD 8.8 billion in 2015-16.

In terms of technologies, more than half of total amount of finance committed to electricity in 2015-16 was related to renewable projects, mainly on-shore wind and solar energy. Although there has been a huge amount of investment in renewable energy technologies, the scaling up global investment requires declining prices for renewables. However, in the same period, investments in coal plants increased in Africa and Asia, from US$2.8 billion in 2013-14 to US$6.8 billion in 2015-16. Philippines, India, Bangladesh and Kenia have received large financing commitments in 2015-16.

Taking into account the global corporate market at the beginning of the 21st century, sustainable or green investments have gone through three stages—Envirotech, Cleantech and Sustaintech (Ge and De Clercq 2017). First, the envirotech stage has been driven by environmental technology in addition to government policy and regulations. Envirotech investments have aimed to address traditional environmental issues, such as solid waste treatment, water treatment and renewable energy. The envirotech business has been characterized by capital intensive investments reliant on scaling up for competitive advantage.

After the emergence of the envirotech stage, cleantech investments have described those green investments driven by technological innovations and cost-reduction. Among other examples, we can highlight solar photovoltaics, electric vehicles, LEDs, batteries, semiconductors, and energy efficiency-related investments. The requirement of long research and development periods in cleantech business models has created high technical barriers for competitors.

The latest evolution of green investments has been defined as the sustaintech stage where digital and cloud based technologies are currently being applied to accelerate sustainable investments through the removal of environmental, energy and resource constraints. Venture Capital investments have successfully funded sustaintech companies through the past several years, such as Opower, Nest, Solarcity and Tesla. While Google acquired Nest for US$3.2 billion in 2014, Oracle acquired Opower for US$532 million in 2016.

Taking into account the new business models, sustaintech firms have shifted towards less capital intensive investments and the proliferation of disruptive technologies. Disruptive technologies are playing a key role in sustainable development, such as the Internet of Things, Artificial Intelligence, Augmented Reality/Virtual Reality, Big Data, 3D Printing and Advanced Material:

- Internet of Things sensor technology is enhancing sustainability with regards to energy efficiency, water resources and transportation.
- Artificial Investment technology, satellite imagery, computational methods are being used to improve predictions to improve agriculture sustainability.
- Virtual Reality and Augmented Reality (AR/VR) technologies have shown signs of potential to transform business processes in a wide range of industries.
- Big Data has been oriented to optimize energy efficiency and to reduce the cost of clean technologies -related to solar panels and electric vehicles, for instance.
- 3D Printing technology can improve resource efficiency in manufacturing and increase the use of green materials.

- Advanced Materials technology can substitute non-renewable resources by recyclable and it can also enable efficiency in power devices.

In addition to the expansion of disruptive technologies, global discussions have revealed the deleterious effects of the main features of contemporary capitalism. First, the commodification of natural resources is a feature of the long-run process of financial expansion characterized as the financialisation of the capitalist economy where social vulnerabilities have increased – mainly in less developed regions. Second, market deregulation opened up new energy investment patterns in a context where institutional investors have assumed an active role in the selection of high profit potential projects. Under the expansion of monopoly-capital, deep concerns have arisen, since energy policies and investments could pass down social and environmental safeguards.

Energy policies, investments and climate finance are closely intertwined. Accordingly the World Bank, climate finance refers to financial resources invested in mitigation and adaptation projects through financial instruments including loans, grants and guarantees (Madi 2017). Today, we can notice a complex climate finance landscape with a set of sources, institutions, instruments, recipients and uses. The supply-side of climate finance shows that the amount of climate finance resources invested in low-carbon and climate-resilient growth has increased in the last decade but there are still not enough.[1] More investments are needed in energy efficiency and low-carbon technologies up to 20130 to meet the Paris Agreement. Article 2.1c of the Paris Agreement includes a long-term ambition to low greenhouse gas emissions.

Today, the outcomes of global climate negotiations reveal many challenges to decarbonize the economies. Indeed, restructuring energy policies to face climate change require comprehensive solutions in order to face financial, educational, political challenges. First, there is the climate finance challenge as private actors are the main actors of the investment

---

[1] For more details see http://www.climatefinancelandscape.org/?gclid=CPKGn6OZ_NMCFQ-AkQod8j4L9A.

process while the governments lead the climate change negotiations. Second, there is the educational challenge both between children, young people and professionals to face the requirements to improve teaching practices towards the environment and disaster risk reduction. Third, there is a mismatch between the actions of the ministries of environment and the ministries of economy and finance all around the world. Indeed, global climate negotiations reveal the lack of articulation between governments and the private sector in the promotion of: i) changes in current investment patterns towards clean energy, and ii) new educational standards towards a green economy.

The articulation of climate finance with governments and private actors might be consistent with 2-degree pathways. Taking into account the global investment landscape, the case for climate action has never been stronger. It is a must to examine carefully this important aspect of our real economies in a way that leads to a better understanding of the current role of:

- Private equity funds as drivers of climate finance projects.
- Private equity funds as drivers of green investments in their portfolio companies.

Energy investments have been increasingly tied to the private sector. As a result, investment banks, asset managers, private equity funds and other institutional investors have key role in the diversification of energy investments. As private equity funds centralize endowments from banks, institutional investors and high net worth individuals, they might assume a key role in these investments.

On a global level, global climate finance flows increased in 2017 and 2018. In this setting, Bloomberg New Energy Finance highlights that renewable investments, including solar PV panels, onshore wind and electric vehicles have expanded their participation in the energy matrix of many countries. China has experienced a rapid increase in sustainable investments over the past several years with strong government policy support and nowadays it is the leader of global renewable investments. As of 2017, giant wind projects spread between the US, Mexico, UK, Germany and Australia.

The average flows across 2015/2016 amounted US$463 billion. The private sector contributed with 42% of total climate finance resources by 2013, 61% in 2014 and 54% annually for 2015/2016. Private actors (Table 45) have mainly financed renewable energy projects, such as solar PV projects in high-income and upper-middle income countries (Japan, the US and China). Indeed, private investments in renewable energy projects have been representing the largest share of the total. Although lower oil prices proved to be a challenge for biofuels in transport and renewable heat, the renewables-based power generation capacity is estimated to continue increasing in wind power (Japan, Korea and China), solar power (China, Japan) and hydropower (IE 2015).

The participation of the public actors (Table 46) fell to 39% in 2014 but it increased to 46% in 2016, mainly because of the investments of governments and national development banks. Indeed, the public sector still plays a relevant role in covering risks and bridging viability gaps regarding climate finance actions. In 2016, public resources have been oriented to renewable energy (US$57 billion), energy efficiency (US$29 billion), transport (US$81 billion) and land use (US$4 billion), adaptation (US$22 billion) and other (US$21 billion).

Moreover, the role of development banks has corresponded to 89% of the total public finance. Indeed, National Development Finance Institutions (DFIs) almost doubled climate finance commitments in 2015/2016 over the 2013/2014 period. Grants from government entities' and Climate Funds' resources have supported projects in low and lower-middle income countries. Public climate finance instruments, such as low-cost loans, have represented the majority of bilateral DFIs' international financing and a significant part of national DFI's domestic financing. In high- and upper-middle income countries, DFIs' low-cost loans have been oriented to mitigation and/or adaptation projects. MDFIs' market-rate loans – often mixed with governments and Climate Funds' concessional resources – have been oriented to sustainable transport and renewable energy generation projects.

In particular, Multilateral Development Banks (MDBs) increased the provision of climate finance to developing countries MDBs and also channeled resources from developed countries to developing countries (UNFCC 2016). Over 2015/2016, according to the Climate Policy Initiative, 81% of finance was raised in the same country in which it was spent, while the non-OECD countries of East Asia and Pacific received 39% of flows, followed by Western Europe (23%) and the OECD countries of Americas (12%). Moreover, risk management instruments have also been provided by multilateral DFIs in order to encompass credit guarantees, political risk insurances, and contingency recovery grants. These risk management instruments can certainly play a relevant role in enhancing private investments while they can back private equity and debt financing in countries with sluggish investment backgrounds.

Table 45. Private climate finance: Sources and actors, 2014-2016

Private Sources oriented to renewables	Main findings
Project Developers: national/regional utilities/independent power producers	These actors are drivers of the largest volume of private finance and increased their spending 61% from 2014 to 2015.
Direct Institutional Investment	Small but growing role.
Commercial financial institutions	Large role.

Source: Climate Policy Imitative (2018).
Note: Institutional investors, such as private equity funds, have been associated with project developers.

In this scenario it is worth remembering that public sources for climate finance have been lower than the amount of government subsidies for fossil fuel consumption that, in 2014, amounted almost US$493 billion (IEA 2015). Climate finance depends on the real underlying costs that, at many times, happen to be damped by subsidies on behalf of political and competitive concerns (Markovich 2012).

Table 46. Public climate finance: Classification of sources and actors

Public Sources	Actors
Governments & agencies	Bilateral Aid Agencies Export Credit Agencies UN Institutions
Development Finance Institutions	Multilateral Development Banks National Development Banks Bilateral Financial Institutions
Climate Funds	Global Environment Policy Adaptation Fund Climate Investment Funds Green Climate Fund

Source: Climate Policy Initiative (2018).

Table 47. Climate finance: Classification of mitigation and adaptation projects

Mitigation	Adaptation
Renewable energy generation	Water supply management
Energy efficiency in industry and buildings	Climate-resilient infrastructure
Sustainable transport	Costal protection
AFOLU & livestock management	Disaster risk reduction
	AFOLU & natural resource management

Source: World Bank.
Note: AFOLU refers to Agriculture, Forestry and other land uses.

Investment projects associated with climate finance mitigation focus the elimination or reduction of climate change long-term risks while projects related to climate finance adaptation privilege the adjustment of the economy/society to climate change short-term outcomes (Table 47). In recent years, most of the investments have been oriented to mitigation projects. According to UNFCC (2016), more than 70% of the public climate finance in developing countries in 2013/2014 was oriented to mitigation projects.

Adaptation finance has been associated to grants, mainly approved by Climate Funds and Bilateral Financial Institutions. Some least developed countries and small developing nations in Africa and Asia have been the largest recipients of adaptation finance in the period between 2013 and 2015.

Developing country governments received about 40% of the total climate finance flows between 2013 and 2014 (UNCC 2016). The analysis of the geographic focus of climate finance showed that Asian and European countries received more than 50% in 2013/ 2014 - mainly China that remained the largest destination, being followed by Western Europe.

Regarding private climate finance, investment projects oriented to adaptation and mitigation have been locally financed by private resources. Among the private equity funds, current strategies related to climate finance mitigation are:

- **Focus on renewable energy investments:** Fund managers are focusing on conventional investments that do not require R&D spending.
- **Increasing fund–raising among pension funds:** Fund managers have increased the financial endowments from pension funds to match liabilities with projects in clean power. For instance, Octopus Investments Ltd. has invested in solar and wind projects.
- **Global market diversification:** Some fund managers are searching investments targets for higher returns in Asia, Latin America and Africa. For example, Terra Firma Capital Partners Ltd. is starting energy projects in Vietnam, Saudi Arabia, Iran, Ghana and Uganda.

Which are the Challenges for Private Equity Investments in Energy Projects in the Near Future?

Among the main challenges, we can highlight:

- The continuity of expansionary monetary policies might foster renewable energy project developers to expand investments.
- Longer holding periods to get the expected returns might estimulate long-term energy investments.
- Tax and regulatory changes might dampen future profitability in energy projects.

Today, comprehensive solutions are required to include regulation and finance, technology and innovation, governance and politics, environmental and social issues. There is the need to overcome the lack of articulation between governments and the private sector so as to promote changes in investment patterns. As long as clean energy investments are capital-intensive and involve long-run planning and operating decisions, any sustainable clean energy pattern requires political compromise, besides the enforceability of contracts and property rights, in a new ethical framework that enhances the scaling up climate finance. For instance, within the PE industry, the Climate Finance Accelerator Luxembourg (ICFA Luxembourg) innovation is dedicated to fund managers and aims to give early-stage support for projects with a high-climate-related impact potential. As of 2018, private equity investments continued relevant in renewables - investment in renewable energy excluding large hydro-electric projects, plus equity-raising by companies in smart grid, digital energy, energy storage and electric vehicles. Indeed, PE investments presented a sharp increase. A among the largest new deals, many of them involved Chinese electric vehicle companies. In this scenario, utilities disclosed almost US$7 billion in venture capital, private equity and merger and acquisition deals in 2017, according to Bloomberg New Energy Finance. For instance, Energy Impact Partners LP, which represents big companies such as Southern Co., National Grid Plc and AGL Energy Ltd., invested more than US$200 million in companies like Advanced Microgrid Solutions LLC, AutoGrid Systems Inc. and Tendril Networks Inc.

According to the United Nations Sustainable Development Goal (SDG), clean energy and the eradication of poverty are intertwined. Overall, the effectiveness of climate investment is not the required to face climate change negative outcomes. Therefore, the alignment of PE investments with climate finance adaptation and mitigation projects will be crucial in the next years. In this attempt, private equity actions to shift from high-carbon to low-carbon activities might follow some guiding principles:

- Commitment to face global warming;
- Proactive options (mitigation) must be combined with plans to live with the consequences of global warming (adaptation);
- Allocation of resources must support human rights such as food security and gender equality.

In: Private Equity Globalisation
Editor: M. Madi

ISBN: 978-1-53615-043-8
© 2019 Nova Science Publishers, Inc.

Chapter 8

CONCLUSION: THE END OF PRIVATE EQUITY AS WE KNOW IT?

8.1. REBALANCING ECONOMIC POWER TOWARDS ETHICAL BUSINESS

In the new millennium, the proliferation of financial assets, with unstable economic growth, has given way to widespread to precarious jobs, income gaps and weaker welfare programs. The same policies that have obliterated social services and kept labour cheap have supported the expansion of short-termism and new global business models in the context of deregulated capitalism. The onset of the 21st century represents a new political age overwhelmed by the violation of democratic ideals of political equality and social peace. Indeed, democracy has been allowing for election to office but not to power (Madi 2015). And, as a consequence, policy makers might give priority to their sponsors instead of the needs of citizens – decent work and income equality. At this point it is interesting to recall the analysis of Pierre Dardot and Christian Laval (2013) that highlights that in Western societies there is a set of values spread that supports progress as a 'truth" called *efficiency*. This scenario calls for a serious reflection about the social implications of current scientific and technological trends and the ethical issues that overwhelm the current manifestations of desembedness and the commodification of economics.

In truth, the current trends in global capital accumulation and production have shaped a scenario where unemployment, job instability and fragile conditions of social protection increased (Stiglitz 2012). First, the demand for blue-collar workers has been reduced by labour-saving technologies. Second, in the global market, higher labour costs and regulations foster outsourcing practices. Third, the declining role of unions has affected the bargaining power of workers. Four, political decisions are influenced by the top 1% who privilege policies that increase income inequality.

All these trends do reveal political and economic concerns in a global scenario where democratic institutions are being threatened. Taking into account the overall economic, social and political evidence in Western countries, Robert Kuttner, in his recent 2018 book *Can Democracy Survive Global Capitalism?*, highlights that since the 1970s the globalisation of capital has affected the very foundation of a healthy democracy. Indeed, rethinking the future of the private equity industry involves at least eight challenges that are presented in Figure 3.

Source: Aubourg and Coekelbergs (2018). https://www.lpea.lu/2018/05/31/the-private-equity-industry-time-to-reinvent-itself-or-to-disappear/.

Figure 3. Current Challenges of the Private Equity Industry.

As Madi (2016) highlights, the conceptualization of business sustainability in the context of global competitiveness is relevant to apprehend the challenges for building an inclusive economy. The drivers of sustainability are entrepreneurship, innovation and finance. Business sustainability is anchored in a Schumpeterian approach to innovation and entrepreneurship embodied in a complex learning processes and dynamic networks that drive economic cyclical growth and development.

Business sustainability is also influenced by finance. Keynes' analysis of entrepreneurship and business instability highlights that the dynamics of contemporary finance is mostly based upon conventions whose precariousness could dampen the rhythm of investment. In his view, the expansion of capital markets reinforces the potential conflicts of interest between business strategies that favor short-run and long-run decisions putting pressure on sustainable entrepreneurship. The value of his analysis relies on cultural and social factors since finance, trust and conventions are intertwined.

Throughout the economic cycle, the degree of competitiveness is a key indicator of sustainability. With the deep and rapid changes in the social, financial and technological dimensions of business, many private equity managers have been more inclined to drive innovations to improve profits in favor of cost-cutting. Indeed, cost-reduction practices do not necessarily give competitive advantage to the PE portfolio companies. Thus, it is increasingly important to look for innovations, such as new products, processes and markets that are about to grow in the future.

At the core of current challenges is the conflict between business strategies based on short-run profits, on one side, and those strategies that support long-run investment decisions, on the other. This tension is extremely important today, since the private equity business model has been historically overwhelmed by the financial logic of investment. Looking back, PE managers turned out to focus on short-term profits and performance fees.

Recalling Minsky (1986), in contemporary capitalism, corporate governance needs to be analysed in a framework where the role of finance is outstanding. Managers have been increasingly subordinated strategies to financial commitments and, therefore, finance determines the pace of investment and employment. In truth, over the last decades, the leveraged buyout business model has fostered the financialisation of corporate behaviour. It is relevant to apprehend this recent business trends since the centralization of financial resources by PE funds has arisen deep concerns because of job losses, reduction in incomes, attacks on pension rights and the displacement of workers.

That is why the current global economic and social landscape poses a major challenge to investors, managers and regulators within the private equity industry.

How Will the Private Equity Industry Look Back on 2019 a Decade from Now?

To answer this question, we can recall the fruitful contributions of Elinor Ostrom, the only woman ever to win the Nobel Prize in Economics. In her famous book, *Governing the Commons: The Evolution of Institutions for Collective Action* (1990), she focused on the capacity of groups of people around the globe to create long-run resilient arrangements in order to protect the environmental resources. In particular, she studied how groups manage and preserve common-pool resources such as forests and water supplies. However, collective actions have not inevitably emerged in all groups. She defined common or common-pool resources as public goods with finite benefits. Therefore, common-pool resources can be potentially used beyond the limits of sustainability because of the lack of exclusion of users. This creates an incentive for increasing the rate of use of this resource above its physical or biological renewal. Besides, her research pointed out that common property is a kind of institutional arrangement that regulates ownership and responsibility.

In this framework, Ostrom developed a theoretical approach to the management of common-pool resources at local and global levels where polycentric systems of governance refer to build collective-actions. In this respect, she concluded there is not one ideal governance regime, but a variety of regimes of governance that might include: rules of appropriation and maintenance of resources, rules of conflict resolution and the evaluation of strategies to change rules. Indeed, the users of common-pool resource can work together to enhance the sustainable governance of their commons by collective action. Indeed, under her view, successful commons' self-governance institutional arrangements depend on: the coherence between the resource environment and its self-government structure, the enforcement of rules through effective monitoring and sanctions, and the adoption of low-cost conflict resolution mechanisms.

According to Ostrom, adaptive governance is related to changing rules and enforcement mechanisms over time since institutional arrangements are able to cope with human and natural complex systems. As a result, citizens, governments and businessmen might deal with collective-action problems in different ways at diverse scales. Indeed, her contribution adds to our understanding how collective actions and polycentric arrangements of governance can influence economic outcomes, human behaviours and institutions towards growing resilience and sustainability. In this attempt, she crossed traditional boundaries between political science and economics. Indeed, Olstrom's proposal is at the core of ethical business in a Pragmatist perspective that certainly offers to us a new way of looking at institutions in real world societies. In fact, the fundamental problem in economics is the attendance of human needs. This approach is supported by ethical principles that touch on social justice.

8.2. From Short-Termism to a Long-Run Responsible Perspective

Finance is not just related to management techniques, procedures or product phenomena but involve institutions, behaviours and policies. In a monetary economy, accordingly John Maynard Keynes, money, as the institution that founds the exchange system, is a link between the present and the future. Finance fosters the capital accumulation process that develops through time and involves credit contracts. From the Keynesian tradition, Hyman Minsky (1986) argued that finance could be apprehended in a changing historical framework where arise tensions between regulation and the strategies of innovative profit-seeking banks. In this scenario, financial innovations, such as private equity funds, provoke changes in market dynamics on behalf of the interconnections between credit and capital markets on one side, and the good and services markets on the other.

Deregulated finance has been associated to great transformations in the models of economic growth. Accordingly Stockhammer (2009), the notion of a "finance dominated" accumulation regime highlights that the current global financial set up has decisively shaped a pattern of accumulation where different growth models could be identified. While some countries have presented a consumption-driven growth model fueled by credit, generally followed by current account deficits, other countries have shown an export-driven growth model, mainly characterized by modest consumption growth and large current account surpluses.

In spite of the coexistence of different growth models, the financial-led accumulation regime has presented some distinctive features:

- A redefinition of the role of the state that has been justified by the deregulation process in financial, product and labour markets.
- Changes in macroeconomic policies that turned out to focus fiscal adjustments instead of employment goals.
- The centralization of capital, trough waves of M&A and the expansion of sub-contracting schemes (outsourcing) have been nurtured by short-term profit goals. In fact, one of the most important changes in investment decisions resulted from the increased pressure of shareholders. Assets, debts, current stock market evaluation, mergers and acquisitions have overwhelmed the practice of investment decisions. Indeed, the financial conception of investment has been spread in a context where financial innovations (debt and securities) have been used to achieve fast growth with lower capital requirements.
- The redefinition of labour and working conditions that has been at the center of increasing inequality. In truth, the evolution of the

capitalist relations of production has revealed changing labour organizing principles in order to cope with the dictates of capital mobility and competition: automatic production control, redefinition of workers' skills and tasks in the context of new management practices, job rotation and suppression of rights. Moreover, attacks on trade unions and the diminishing strength of collective demands need to be underlined. In this context, the deterioration of income distribution and the weak perspectives of job creation are continuously putting a downward pressure on consumption and, therefore, on economic growth.

Indeed, these world-wide evidences reinforced deep menaces to social cohesion and justice in the context of the current financial-led accumulation regime. Because of these menaces, Eric Hobsbawm (2007, 137) sharply notes that: "They seem to reflect the profound social dislocations brought about at all levels of society by the most rapid and dramatic transformation in human life and society experienced within single lifetimes. They also seem to reflect both a crisis in traditional systems of authority, hegemony and legitimacy in the west and their breakdown in the east and the south, as well as a crisis in the traditional movements that claimed to provide an alternative to these."

The interconnections between power, finance and business governance characterize our approach to business (Madi 2016). While the very nature of wealth management under uncertainty in a monetary economy is the cause of business instability, entrepreneurs might postpone spending decisions and search for alternatives of wealth management. As opposed to the free-market economists that are defenders of laissez faire capitalism, we believe that policies and regulations can play a fundamental role in shaping conventions within the business environment since they are influenced by a set of cultural, institutional, political and economic factors. In the attempt to re-shape global business models, we need a wide measure of agreement that has a historical and social nature and, therefore, this agreement will impact the model of economic growth.

How Can the Gap Between Current Business Governance and Social and Environmental Justice be Bridged?

The answer to this question is not easy since the expansion of neoliberalism in the last five decades has increasingly expressed the tensions between the expansion of the market economy and the consolidation of a new way of life. However, the outstanding insights of Karl Polanyi about the way in which the economy relates to social organization and culture should be addressed in any attempt to bridge the gap between current social and environmental justice and business governance.

Taking into account the current effects of the neoliberal modernization process on lifestyles, Karl Polanyi's critique of the liberal myth and of the disruptive forces inherent to the self-regulated markets is inspiring to rethink the impacts of institutions on livelihoods since the institutional patterns and principles of behaviour turn out to adjust perfectly. Consequently, the neoliberal way of life is an important expression of the recent economic and cultural transformations because new habits of behavior and institutions may possible to enlarge the subordination of sociability conditions to the market economy. Consequently, the social relations increasingly become an "accessory of the economic system" (Polanyi 1944, 75). The beliefs, habits of behaviour and the institutional set up have turned out to privilege competition in social dynamics. In this scenario, the main challenge for the PE industry is to commit investors and managers to long-run social sustainability.

As Polanyi warned, the transformation of individual behaviour towards the economic motive has disorganized the traditional forms of reciprocity and redistribution. As a result, the human way of life has been increasingly subordinated to the commodity fiction (Madi and Gonçalves 2007). As the commodity fiction proves to be the vital organizing process, the self-regulated markets demand the institutional separation of society into an economic and a political sphere. In other words, the commodity fiction implies that the economy is not embedded in the social relations.

Considering the urgence of enhancing social and environmental justice, we can cinclude that the utilization of financial engineering techniques in the private equity business model is not sufficient to overcome current global problems. After some decades, it is a reality that the global economic integration, guided by market credibility and financial rules, has broadened social exclusion. The new interconnections between wealth, production, labour and consumption have strengthened inequalities. Indeed, the apprehension of current global inequality issues involves the understanding of the deep tensions between the hypertrophy of finance in economic dynamics and the expectations of society about citizenship, jobs and income.

To create social value in the near future, private equity managers should develop new strategies. In fact, the transition to a new generation of LPs and GPs is a real challenge since current the largest PE funds are still dependent on the founders (LPEA 2018c). Younger generation believes more in the importance of providing value-add pro-active to portfolio companies against GPs more strictly financial oriented. Younger GPs are increasingly considering new emerging corporate governance trends, like ESG standards – Environmental, Social and Governance, in the context of the PE industry. For instance, the private equity firm PAI Partners has already built a dedicated ESG team. A survey conducted by the Morgan Stanley Institute for Sustainable Investing and Morgan Stanley Investment Management in 2018 revealed that, among 118 institutional asset owners[1], sustainable investing is increasingly.

In the near future, responsible investing might enable investors and managers to think more systematically about risks and costs arising from ESG factors that can affect long-run returns for investors (Figure 4). Nowadays, the perception of a trade-off between good ESG practices and financial performance is being replaced by a business strategy where environmental, social and governance issues can contribute to higher potential returns. Indeed, among social and governance concerns, the commodification of natural resources puts pressure on urgent climate change actions.

Among the 118 institutional asset owners: 20 from North America, 67 from Europe and 31 from Asia. More details in Morgan Stanley (2018). https://www.morganstanley.com/assets/pdfs/sustainable-signals-asset-owners-2018-survey.pdf.

Source: Adapted from LPEA (2018d).

Figure 4. Private Equity Responsible Investing

Changes in business conventions towards responsible investment rely on norms, expectations and actions that could favor long-run investments with inclusiveness. Today, innovation, finance and knowledge provide new parameters for PE strategies and decision-making. Actually, managers need to access external new sources of information, knowledge and technologies, in order to build their own innovative capability and to reach new markets and costumers.

In the global context, the search for responsible investment should not be separated from social and economic development. Private equity responsible investment should be a key feature of the reorganization of social interactions in the near future. It involves the adoption of global guidelines and values to create new ethical practices in business culture. The aim is to modify the relationships among investors, managers, employees, clients, communities and governments. As a result, the private equity industry is expected to be active in protecting the market society.

Indeed, the debate about the role of private equity funds in promoting economic and social development through the benefits of new ethical strategies and practices has been deepened in the aftermath of the global crisis. The participation of private equity funds in the solution of social, economic and environmental challenges might create new forms of social protection in a globalized market system.

In this scenario, the role of policy makers and regulators is outstanding to stimulate new business conventions. Table 48 highlights some ideas for scaling up responsible investments. The poposed agenda is organized by topics of interest, mainly finance, innovation and knowledge.

Table 48. Agenda for scaling up private equity responsible investments: Finance, innovation and knowledge

Topics of interest	Actions required
Finance	• Regulation and monitoring of leverage levels. • Monitoring of financial risk management. • Creation of indicators for assessing the effectiveness of responsible investments. • Reform of the tax system.
Innovation	• Greater Integration between PE business, mainly PE venture capital, universities and research centers. • Creation of technological incubators among PE portfolio companies.
Knowledge	• Development of digital transformation in PE portfolio companies. • Generation of more and better jobs. • Building ESG teams. • Creation of indicators for assessing the effectiveness of regulations to the PE industry

Source: Elaborated by the author.

However, so far, private equity strategies and practices related to responsible investment have not overcome the tensions inherent to the organization of the global market society. While short-term portfolio decisions predominate in PE business, the search for increasing efficiency will not be able to defeat inequalities. In this setting, the demand for increasing productivity, instead of serving the human purposes, became the own finality of business. As a result, productivity and efficiency targets are transformed into social exclusion, while the threats against the environment show other deleterious features of global financial power.

When we analyse the relationship between responsible investment and social justice, the contribution of Karl Polanyi to the analysis of the problem of production and distribution in a market society is inspiring to deeply think about the impacts of neoliberal policies on livelihood conditions. In the *Great Transformation*, Polanyi highlighted the challenges to social justice and showed that the dehumanization of capitalism is a result of the particular institutional set up of the market society. It is worth remembering that the current PE business set up embodies the economic motive as an expression of cultural practices and habits of behavior spread in the context of financialisation. The main driven-force of global dynamics has been related to the spread of the culture of money. In this scenario, the political dominance of high finance shaped new elites and cultural practices. This process turned out to enhance the loss of social cohesion since reciprocity in human interrelations has been substituted by individual claims.

Indeed, current business models dramatically impact on society since the spread of market-based values turns to "disjoint man's relationships and threaten his natural habitat with annihilation" (Polanyi 1944, 44). Remembering Polanyi's words: "(...) the control of the economic system by the market is of overwhelming consequence to the whole organization of society: it means no less than the running of society as an adjunct to the market. Instead of economy being embedded in social relations, social relations are embedded in the economic system. ... society must be shaped in such a manner as to allow that system to function according to its own laws. This is the meaning of the familiar assertion that a market economy can function only in a market society" (Polanyi 1944, 60).

The spread of the economic motive is not compatible with responsible investment and social justice. According to Polanyi, these goals "must become chosen aims of the societies towards which we are moving" (Polanyi 1944, 263). In truth, the aims of responsible investment and social justice need to promote a human-based and community-oriented cultural process that is open to changing beliefs, habits of behavior and values to protect society. In short, Polany's ideal of social justice can be summarized in the following words: "The economy has to serve society, not the other way around". Thus, his contribution opens up new perspectives to think about ethics in currrent business against the utilitarian view that overwhelmed the contemporary market society. Taking into account the historical and institutional analysis of capitalism enhanced by Polanyi, an outstanding idea to include in any *ethically* defensible approach to the future of the Private Equity business model is that any transformation in institutional patterns should adjust perfectly to principles of behaviour. Indeed, it is time both to change habits of behaviour within the private equity industry in order to promote responsible investment.

Looking backward to our initial thoughts in Chapter 1, we can now address that the decisive issue at stake is that economics should be reconciled with ethics in a Pragmatist approach. If economic and social changes are authentically "human centered", they need to make room for habits of belief that enhance not only economic growth but also social and environmental justice. Indeed, changes in habits of belief need to be oriented towards the pursuit of the common good for the whole society.

We believe that new habits of belief in business and society should encourage economic transformations. Basically, what is needed is an effective shift in ethical concerns that can lead to the adoption of new business models as mechanisms of "self-protection" in society. A society is a living organism whose *ethos* is the result of a complex combination of customs, norms, beliefs, habits. Indeed, it is not any ethics whatsoever, but an ethics which is people-centered. The centrality of the dignity of human beings is at the heart of the Pragmatist ethical values and these should guide private equity responsible investing towards social and environmental justice.

REFERENCES

On Financialisation and Private Equity Funds

Aldatmaz, S. & Brown, G. W. (2013). "Does Private Equity Hurt or Help the Economy?." *Research Paper, Private equity research Consortium*, Kenan-Flagler Business School, The University of North Carolina at Chapel Hill, March.

Alvarez, Nick. & Jenkins, Richard. (2007). "Private Equity's new Frontier: Operational Investing." *Journal of Private Equity*, *10* (2), 27-29.

Amadeo, Kimberley. (2018). "Long-Term Capital Management Hedge Fund Crisis." *The Balance*.

Amess, K. & Wright, M. (2010). Leveraged buyouts, private equity and jobs. *Small Business Economics*, *29*(3), 329-349.

Amess, K. & Wright, M. (2007). The wage and employment effects of leveraged buyouts in the U.K. *International Journal of Economics and Business.*, *14*(2), 179-195.

Amicus. (2007). *Memorandum of Evidence to Treasury Select Committee Inquiry into Private Equity.* Accessed February 28, 2008. http://www.ituc-csi.org/IMG/pdf/WEF_Statement_-_Labour_and_the_Shifting_Power_Equation_-_Rev_EN.pdf.

Arbaut, Yannik. (2018). *"Fund Structuring – Issuing Tokens In A Fund."* Luxembourg Private Equity Association (LPEA). Accessed December

2, 2018. https://www.lpea.lu/wp-content/uploads/2018/02/ peinsightout
-v9-md-pp.pdf.

Appelbaum, E., Batt, R. & Clarke, I. (2013). "Implications of Financial
Capitalism for Employment Relations Research: Evidence from Breach
of Trust and Implicit Contracts in Private Equity Buyouts". *British
Journal of Industrial Relations.* Accessed October 10, 2015.
http://onlinelibrary.wiley.com/doi/10.1111/bjir.12009/full.

Appelbaum, E. & Batt, R. (2014). *Private Equity at Work: When Wall Street
Manages Main Street.* United States: Russell Sage Foundation.
Accessed October 10, 2015. http://www.ituc-csi.org/IMG/pdf/WEF_
Statement_-_Labour_and_the_Shifting_Power_Equation_-_Rev_EN.
pdf.

Ayash, B. & Rastad, M. (2017). "Private equity, jobs, and productivity: A
comment." October. *SSRN.* https://ssrn.com/abstract=305098.

Aubourg, Jose. & Coekelbergs, Olivier. "The Private Equity Industry: Time
To Reinvent Itself Or To Disappear." 2018. *Private Equity Insight, 1.*
Luxembourg Private Equity Association. Accessed December 20, 2018.
https://www.lpea.lu/2018/05/31/the-private-equity-industry-time-to-
reinvent-itself-or-to-disappear/.

Bacon, N., Wright, M., Demina, N., Bruining, H. & Boselie, P. (2008). "The
effects of private equity and buy-outs on HRM in the UK and the
Netherlands." *Human Relations, 61*(10), 1399-1433.

Bain & Company. (2014). *Global Private Equity Report 2014.* USA: Bain
&Company, Inc.Bain & Company. 2015. *Global Private Equity Report
2015.* USA: Bain &Company, Inc.

Bain & Company. (2017). *Global Private Equity Report 2017.* USA: Bain
&Company, Inc.

Bain & Company. (2018 a). *Global Private Equity Report 2018.* USA: Bain
&Company, Inc.

Bain & Company. (2018b). *Asia-Pacific Private Equity Report.* USA: Bain
& Company, Inc. Accessed January 5, 2019. https://www.bain.com/
insights/asia-pacific-private-equity-report-2018/.

Bank of International Settlement (BIS). (2008). "Private equity and
leveraged finance markets." *Committee on the Global Financial System*

Papers, *30*. Accessed March 30, 2009. http://www.bis.org/publ/cgfs30.pdf?noframes=.1.

Bank of International Settlement (BIS). (2012). "Post-crisis evolution of the banking sector", In *BIS 82nd Annual Report*, Basel: BIS. Accessed June 25, 2013. http://www.bis.org/publ/arpdf/ar2012e6.pdf.

Bauman, Zygmunt. (2000). *Liquid Modernity*. USA: Polity Press.

Bello, Wladen. (2004). *Deglobalization: ideas for a new world economy.* Chicago: Chicago University Press.

Bloomberg New Energy Finance. (2017). *"Green technologies get boost from EU's venture capital funds."* Accessed May 10, 2018. https://about.bnef.com/blog/green-technologies-get-boost-from-eus-venture-capital-funds/.

Blum, R. (2008). *Leveraged buyouts, private equity and restructuring in the metal sector.* Special Report. Metal World, Accessed March 31, 2009. http://www.imfmetal.org/files/08090411533679/special_report. pdf.

Braadbaart, L. (2018). *2017 sixth consecutive year of pension fund growth, UK*: Moneyfacts. https://moneyfacts.co.uk/news/pensions/2017-sixth-consecutive-year-of-pension-fund-growth/.

Broadbent, J., Palumbo, M. & Woodman, E. (2006). The Shift from Defined Benefit to Defined Contribution Pension Plans – Implications for Asset Allocation and Risk Management. *Paper prepared for a Working Group on Institutional Investors, Global Savings and Asset Allocation established by the Committee on the Global Financial System*, BIS.

Brigl, Michael., Jansen, Axel., Schwetzler, Bernhard., Hammer, Benjamin. & Hinrichs, Heiko. (2016). "How Private Equity Firms Fuel Next-Level Value Creation." *BCG.* Accessed on January 5, 2019. https://www.bcg.com/publications/2016/private-equity-power-of-buy-build.aspx.

British Venture Capital Association. BVCA. (2005). *The economic impact of Private Equity in the UK 2005.* Report. London: British Venture Capital Association.

British Venture Capital Association. BVCA Academic Research Portal. www.bvca.co.uk.

British Venture Capital Association. BVCA. (2017). *Annual Report on the performance of portfolio companies.* December. BVCA 10th edition. Accessed December 10, 2018. https://www.bvca.co.uk/Portals/0/Documents/Research/2017%20Reports/EY-Annual-Report-on-the-Performance-of-Portfolio-Companies-X-Dec-17-IV.pdf?ver=2018-02-13-111903-593&timestamp=1518520807338.

British Venture Capital Association. BVCA. (2018). *Women in Private Equity.* BVCA and Level 20. Accessed January 15, 2109. https://www.bvca.co.uk/Portals/0/Documents/Research/2018%20Reports/BVCA-Women-in-PE-Report-2018.pdf?ver=2018-05-23-141953-723&timestamp=1527081597528.

Burrough, Bryan. & Helyar, John. (1989). *Barbarians at the Gate: The Fall of RJR Nabisco.* Harvard Business Essentials.

Carey, B. (2016). "Cleaned up, shrunken banking sector may now be too small." *The Sunday Times*, August 7th. Accessed September 10, 2018. http://www.thetimes.co.uk/article/cleaned-up-shrunken-banking-sector-may-now-be-too-small-76mwtdvvx.

Çelik, S. & Isaksson, M. (2013). "Institutional Investors as Owners: Who Are They and What Do They Do?." *OECD Corporate Governance Working Papers, 11*, France: OECD Publishing. Accessed October 10, 2015. http://dx.doi.org/10.1787/5k3v1dvmfk42-en.

Cho, David. (2007). *"Nasdaq gives high rollers a market free of regulation."* *Washington Post*, August 13h.

Clark, G. L. (1999). "The retreat of the state and the rise of pension fund capitalism." In *Money and the space economy* edited by R. Martin. Chichester: Wiley.

Clark, I. (2013). "Templates for Financial Control: Management and Employees under Private Equity." *Human Resource Management Journal, 23*(2), 144-159.

Clark. G. I. (2009). "Private equity in the UK: Job regulation and trade unions." *Journal of Industrial Relations, 51*(4), 489-500.

Clark, G. I. (2007). "Private Equity and HRM in the British Business System." *Human Resource Management Journal, 17*(3), 218-226.

Climate Policy Initiative. (2018). *Climate policy Report*. Accessed January 10, 2019. http://www.climatefinancelandscape.org/.

Cressy, R., Munari, F. & Malipiero, A. (2007). "Creative destruction? UK Evidence that buyouts cut jobs to raise returns." *Working Paper Series*. Accessed October 10, 2015. http://ssrn.com/abstract=1030830.

Crotty, J. (2002). "The effects of increased product market competition and changes in financial markets on the performance of nonfinancial corporations in the neoliberal era." *Working Paper Series, 44*. University of Massachusetts Amherst, Political Economy Research Institute.

Cullen, A. & James, S. (2007). "Private equity and Business Information. Part 3: Business Information Services and Private equity: North American Involvement." *Business Information Alert, 19*(10), 1-4.

Cumming, D., Fleming, G. & Johan, S. (2011). "Institutional investment in listed private equity." *European Financial Management, 17*(3), 594-618.

Dardot, P. & Laval, Christian. (2013). *The New Way of the World: On Neoliberal Society*. New York: Gregory Elliott London.

Davis, S., Haltiwanger, J., Jarmin, R., Lerner, J. & Miranda, J. (2008). "Private Equity and Employment." *Working Papers*, 08-07, Center for Economic Studies, US Census Bureau.

Deloitte. (2013). *Private Equity: structures for investing in China*. 2014/2015 edition Deloitte tax research foundation. Accessed January 5, 2019. https://www2.deloitte.com/content/dam/ Deloitte/cn/ Documents/tax/deloitte-cn-tax-private-equity-structures-for-investing-china-en-060114.pdfhttps://www2.deloitte.com/content/dam/Deloitte/cn/Documents/tax/deloitte-cn-tax-private-equity-structures-for-investing-china-en-060114.pdf.

Dermine, J. & Bissada, Y. (2007). *Asset and Liability Management: The Banker's Guide to Value Creation and Risk Control*, London and New York: Financial Times and Prentice Hall.

Diller, Christian. & Jäckel, Christoph. (2015). Risk in Private Equity. New insights into the risk of a portfolio of private equity funds. Montana Capital Partners. *BVCA Research Paper*, October. Accessed January 8,

2019. https://www.bvca.co.uk/Portals/0/library/documents/ Guide%20to%20Risk/Risk%20in%20Private%20Equity%20-%20Oct%20 2015.pdf?ver=2015-10-07-112204-040.

Dixon, H., Cox, R. & Chancellor, E. (2007). "Conglomerate Comparisons – Will Private- Equity Empires Parallel Predecessors of 1960s and Fall Out of Fashion Too?." *Wall St. Journal*, January 2, C12.

Diversity, V. C. & BVCA. (2017). *Women in UK venture capital 2017.* Accessed January 15, 2019. http://www.diversity.vc/women-in-uk-vc/.

Emirdag, Pinar. (2018). *Cryptoassets Are Likely To Become Part Of Thefund Landscape.* LPEA, Accessed Decemebr 20, 2018. https:// www.lpea.lu/wp-content/uploads/2018/02/peinsightout-v9-md-pp.pdf.

Ernst & Young. (2016). *Private Equity Survey.* https://www.ey.com.

Ernst & Young. (2018). *Global Corporate Divestment Study.* https://www. ey.com.

Fullbrook, Edward. (2011). "Of the 1%, by the 1%, for the 1%". *RWER Blog*, April 13. https://rwer.wordpress.com/2011/04/13/%E2% 80%9 Cof-the-1-by-the-1-for-the-1%E2%80%9D-joseph-e-stiglitz.

Fligstein, Neill. (2001). *The architecture of markets.* New Jersey: Princeton University Press.

Foster, John Bellamy. (2006). "Monopoly-Finance Capital." *Monthly Review*, *58*, 1-14.

Folkman, P., Froud, Julie., Johal, Sukhdev. & Williams, Karel. (2007). Working for themselves: Financial intermediaries and present day capitalism. *Business History*, *49*(4), 552-572.

Froud, Julie., Haslam, C., Johal, Sukhdev. & Williams, Karel. (2000). "Restructuring for shareholder value and its implications for labour." *Cambridge Journal of Economics*, *24*(6), pp. 771-787.

Froud, Julie., Sukhdev, Johal., Leaver, Adam. & Williams, Karel. (2006). *Financialisation and Strategy. Narrative and Numbers.* London: Routledge.

Froud, Julie. & Williams, Karel. (2007a). "Private equity and the culture of value extraction." *New Political Economy*, *12*, 405-4.

Froud, Julie. & Williams, Karel. (2007b). "New actors in a financialized economy and the remaking of capitalism." *New Political Economy, 12,* 339-347.

Galbraith, James. (2015). *The end of normal.* Simon & Schuster.

GAO. United States Government Accountability Office. (2008). "Private Equity. Recent Growth in Leveraged Buyouts Exposed Risks That Warrant Continued Attention." *GAO-08-885 report to congressional requesters.* Washingrton, DC. September.

Glattfelder, James. (2012). *Decoding Complexity: Uncovering Patterns in Economic Networks.* UK: Springer.

Glossary of Private Equity and Venture Capital Terms. (2019). Allenlatta. http://www.allenlatta.com/glossary-of-private-equity-terms.html.

Gnos, Claude. (2006). "French Circuit Theory." In *A Handbook of Alternative Monetary Economics* edited by Paul Arestis and Malcon Sawyer, Cheltenahm, UK and Northampton, MA, USA: Edward Elgar Publishing, pp. 87-104.

Goergen, M., O'Sullivan, N. & Wood, G. (2011). "Private Equity Takeovers and Employment in the UK." *Corporate Governance: An International Review, 19* (1), 259-275.

Goergen, Marc., O'Sullivan, Noel. & Wood, Geoffrey. (2014). *"The Consequences of Private Equity Acquisitions for Employees: New Evidence on the Impact on Wages, Employment and Productivity."* Research Paper. Accessed December 10, 2018. repository.essex.ac.uk/15441/1/HRMJGoer%20genHRMJ%20-%20accepted%20-%20post-review%20paper.pdf.

Gonçalves, José R. Barbosa. & Madi, Maria A. Caporale. (2011). "Private equity investment and labour: faceless capital and the challenges to trade unions in Brazil." In *Trade unions and the global crisis: Labour's visions, strategies and responses* edited by M Serrano et al. Geneve: Intenational Labour Office.

Gospel, Howard., Pendleton, Andrew. & Vitols, Sigurt. (2013). *Financialisation, New Investment Funds, and Labour – An International Comparison.* Oxford: Oxford University Press.

Hammoud, Tawfic., Brigl, Michael., Öberg, Johan., Bronstein, David. & Carter, Christy. (2017). *Capitalizing on the New Golden Age in Private Equity.* March. Accessed December 10, 2018. https://www.bcg.com/ en-ca/publications/2017/value-creation-strategy-capitalizing-on-new-golden-age-private-equity.aspx.

Harris, R., Siege, D. S. & Wright, M. (2005). "Assessing the impact of management buyouts on economic efficiency: plant-level evidence from the United Kingdom." *The Review of Economics and Statistics, 87*(1), 148-153.

Harvey, David. (2007). *A Brief History of Neoliberalism.* Oxford: Oxford University Press.

Heberlein, Anuar. (2018). *"Private Equity Outlook 2017: Signs of Fatigue."* Toptal. https://www.toptal.com/finance/private-equity-consultants/ private -equity-industry.

Howe, J. (2006). *"The Rise of Crowdsourcing."* Wired. 14 (6). Accessed March 30, 2014. http://www.wired.com/wired/archive/14.06/ crowds. html.

Heerwagen, Judith. (2016). *The Changing Nature of Organizations, Work, And Workplace.* US General Services Administration.

Hill, James. M. & Gambaccini, John. S. (2003). "The Private Equity Paradox: When Is Too Much Control a Bad Thing?." *Journal of Private Equity, 6* (3).

Hobsbawm, Eric. (1995). *The Age of Extremes: a History of the World, 1914-1991,* New York: Pantheon Books.

Hobsbawm, Eric. (2007). *Globalisation, Democracy and Terrorism.* London: Little, Brown.

Ietto-Gillies, Grazia. (2011). "The internationalization of production systems. Implications for firms, labour and countries: The global environment of business," *International Review of Applied Economics, 25*(2), 239-244.

Industry all Global Union. (2011). *"Global Unions demand policy change in finance institutions."* Accessed June 10, 2015. http:// www.industriall-union.org/archive/imf/global-unions-demand-policy-change-in-finance-institutions.

International Union of Food, Agricultural, Hotel, Restaurant, Catering, Tobacco and Allied Workers' Association. IUF. (2009a) *"The IUF's Private Equity Buyout Watch."*, Newsletter, 5 May. Accessed June 10, 2015. http://www.iufdocuments.org/buyoutwatch/2008/05/ global_ credit_crisis_record_20.html.

International Union of Food, Agricultural, Hotel, Restaurant, Catering, Tobacco and Allied Workers' Association. IUF. (2007). *A Workers'Guide to private Equity Buyouts*. Geneve.

International Union of Food, Agricultural, Hotel, Restaurant, Catering, Tobacco and Allied Workers' Association.IUF. 2008. *Private Equity Buyouts: A Trade Union View*. Geneve.

ITUC- CSI. (2007). *Labour and the Shifting Power Equation: Statement of Labour Leaders to the World Economic Forum Annual Meeting Davos*, Report.

Invest Europe and KPMG (2018). *Tax Benchmark Study 2018: Defining tax environments for the private*. Report. https://www.investeurope.eu/ media/722513/ie_tax-benchmark-study-2018.pdf.

Jacoby, S. (2008). *"Finance and Labour: Perspectives on Risk, Inequality and Democracy." Working Paper*, Institute for Research on Labour and Employment, USA: California Digital Library. Accessed March 31, 2009. http://www.ituc-csi.org/IMG/pdf/WEF_Statement_-_Labour_ and_ the_Shifting_Power_Equation_-_Rev_EN.pdf.

Ipeirotis, P. (2012). *The (Unofficial) NIST Definition of Crowdsourcing*. [Online]. Available: http://www.behind-the-enemy-lines.com/search?q =cloudmechanical-turk-demographics.html.

Jensen, M. (1989). "The eclipse of public corporation." *Harvard Business Review*. Sept.-Oct.

Jensen, M. (2007). "The Economic Case for Private Equity (and Some Concerns)." *Harvard NOM Working Paper* No. 07-02, Swedish Institute for Financial Research Conference on The Economics of the Private Equity Market. Accessed October 10, 2015. http://ssrn.com/ abstract=963530.

Kaplan, Steven. (1989). "The effects of management buyouts on operating performance and value." *Journal of Financial Economics.*, *24*(2), 217-254.

Kaplan, Steven N. & Schoar, Antoinette. (2003). "Private Equity Performance: Returns, Persistence and Capital Flows." *MIT Sloan Working Paper* No. 4446-03, AFA 2004 San Diego Meetings. Accessed October 10, 2015. http://ssrn.com/abstract=473341.

Kelly, Jason. (2007). "Madison Dearbon Beats Blackstone, Goldman Sachs as Deals Stall." *Bloomberg*, Oct 1.

Keynes, John Maynard. [1936 (1964)]. *The General Theory of Employment, Interest, and Money*. New York: Harcourt Brace.

Klier, D., Welge, M. & Harrigan, K. (2009). "The Changing Fface of Private Equity: How Modern Private Equity Firms Manage Investment Portfolios." *Journal of Private Equity*, *12* (4).

Kuttner, Robet. *Can Democracy Survive Global Capitalism?*. WW Norton.

Lavoie, M. (2004). "Circuit and Coherent Stock-Flow Accounting." In *Money, Credit and the Role of the State. Essays in Honor of Augusto Graziani* edited by R. Arena and N. Salvadori. Aldershot: Ashgate.

Lazonick, W. & O'Sullivan, M. (2000). "Maximizing shareholder value: a new ideology for corporate governance." *Economy and Society*, *29* (1).

Luxembourg Private Equity Association (LPEA). (2018). *Insight Out.* Accessed December 2, 2018. https://www.lpea.lu/wp-content/uploads/2018/02/peinsightout-v9-md-pp.pdf.Lichtenberg.

Luxembourg Private Equity Association (LPEA). (2018a). *Thermometer. Newsletter.* Accessed December 2, 2018. https://www.lpea.lu/wp-content/uploads/2018/04/lpea-thermometer-april-2018.pdf.

Luxembourg Private Equity Association (LPEA). (2018b). *Insight Out.* Accessed December 2, 2018. https://www.lpea.lu/2018/02/16/private-equity-insight-out-issue-1-2018/.

Luxembourg Private Equity Association (LPEA). (2018c). *Insight out.* Accessed December 2, 2018. https://www.lpea.lu/2018/09/27/a-new-generation-takes-over/.

Luxembourg Private Equity Association (LPEA). (2018d). *LPEA Insights. Building the real economy*. Accessed December 2, 2018. http://lpea.

wildapricot.org/resources/Documents/LPEA%20Insights%202018_sha
re.pdf.

F. & Siegel, D. (1990). "The effects of leveraged buyouts on productivity
and related aspects of firm behaviour." *Journal of Financial Economics*,
27(1), 165-194.

Madi, Maria A. Caporale. (2016). *Small Business in Brazil: Competitive
Global Challenges*. New York: Nova Science Publishers.

Madi, Maria A. Caporale. (2015). "2016: Promises and Problems." *WEA
Pedagogy Blog*, December 29. https://weapedagogy.wordpress.com/
2015/12/29/2016-promises-and-problems.

Madi, Maria. A. Caporale. (2014). *Global Finance and Development*. India:
Sanbun Publishers.

Madi, Maria A. Caporale. (2013). *"Ethics and Economics." WEA Pedagogy
Blog*, November 10. https://weapedagogy.wordpress.com/ 2013/11/10/
ethics-and-economics/.

Madi, Maria A. Caporale. & Gonçalves, José R. Barbosa. (2007). "Corporate
Social Responsibility and Market Spciety: Credit and Social Exclusion
in Contemporary Brazil." In A. Bugra and K. Agartan. *Reading Karl
Polanyi for the Twenty-First Century: Market Economy as a Political
Project*. UK: Palgrave McMillan.

Madi, Maria A. Caporale. (2016). *Small Business in Brasil: competitive
global challenges*. NY: Nova Science Publishers.

Madi, Maria A. Caporale. (2017a). *Pluralist Readings in Economics: key-
concepts and policy-tools for the 21st century*, Book Series: Economics:
Current and Future Developments, vol. 2. Bentham Publishers.

McKinsey. (2018). "The rise and rise of private markets." *McKinsey Global
Private Markets Review*. Accessed December 20, 2018.
https://www.mckinsey.com/~/media/mckinsey/industries/private%20e
quity%20and%20principal%20investors/our%20insights/the%20rise%
20and%20rise%20of%20private%20equity/the-rise-and-rise-of-
private-markets-mckinsey-global-private-markets-review-2018.ashx.

Metrick, A. & Yasuda, A. (2007). *The Economics of Private Equity Funds*,
US: Wharton School, University of Pennsylvania.

Minsky, Hyman P. (1986). *Stabilizing and Unstable Economy*. Yale University Press.

Montgomerie, J. (2008). "Labour and the Locusts: Private Equity's Impact on the Economy and the Labour Market." *Conference Report of the Seventh British-German Trades Union Forum*, London: Anglo-German Foundation for the Study of Industrial Society.

Morgan, Stanley. (2018). *Sustainable Signals: Asset Owners Embrace Sustainability*. Survey Report. Accessed January 10, 2019. https://www.morganstanley.com/assets/pdfs/sustainable-signals-asset-owners-2018-survey.pdf.

Morgenstein, M., Nealis, P. & Kleinman, K. (2004). "*Going private: a reasoned response to Sarbanes- Oxley?.*" Accessed September 10, 2009. www.sec.gov/info/smallbus/pnealis.pdf.

Ouye, Joe. (2011). *Five Trends That Are Dramatically Changing Work and the Workplace Knoll Workplace Research*. Accessed September 10, 2012. http://www.knoll.com/research/downloads/WP_FiveTrends. pdf.

Pappas, G., Allen, I. & Schalock, A. (2009). "Why Private Equity are Restructuring (and not just their portfolio companies)." *Journal of Private Equity*, *12* (4).

Passarella, M. V. (2014). "Financialisation and the Monetary Circuit: A Macro-accounting Approach." *Review of Political Economy*, *26* (1).

Pearce, Diana. (1978). "The feminization of poverty: women, work, and welfare." *Urban and Social Change Review*, Special Issue: Women and Work, *11* (1-2), 28–36.

Peterman, S. & Lai, D. (2009). "From The Ashes Risen: Private Equity Secondary Funds Take Flight." *Journal of Private Equity.*, *12* (4).

Philips, K. (2006). *American Theocracy: The Peril and Politics of Radical Religion, Oil, and Borrowed Money in the 21st Century*. New York: Viking.

Piketty, T. (2014). *Capital in the 21st century*. Boston: Harvard University Press.

Pilkington, M. (2009). "The financialisation of modern economies in monetary circuit theory." In *The Political Economy of Monetary*

Circuits. Tradition and Change in Post-Keynesian economics edited by J. F. Ponsot and Sergio Rossi. Basingstoke: Palgrave Macmillan.

Polanyi, Karl. [1944(1971)]. *The Great Transformation.* Beacon Press: Boston.

Popper, N. & Corkery, M. (2016). "Shrunken Citigroup Illustrates a Trend in Big U.S. Banks. *New York Time*, April 15, Accessed March 10, 2018. http:// www.nytimes.com/ 2016/ 04/ 16/ business/ dealbook/ shrunken-citigroup-illustrates-a-trend-in-big-us-banks.html.

Preqin Equity on line. www.preqin.com.

Prequin. (2007). *Private Equity Spotlight.* Newsletter. October.

Preqin. (2015). *Prequin Private Equity & Venture Capital Report.* Accessed October 10, 2015. https://www.preqin.com/docs/reports/ 2015-Preqin-Global-Private-Equity-and-Venture-Capital-Report-Sample-Pages.pdf.

Preqin. (2016). *Investor Interview*, June. Accessed December 10, 2018. https://www.toptal.com/finance/private-equity-consultants/private-equity-industry.

Preqin. (2017). *Global Private Equity & Venture Capital Report.* www.preqin.com.

Preqin. (2017 a). *Alternative Assets Performance Monitor.* www.preqin.com.

Preqin. (2017 b). *Preqin Special Report: The Private Equity Top 100*, Feb, Accessed December 10, 2018. http://docs.preqin.com/reports/Preqin-Special-Report-The-Private-Equity-Top-100-February-2017.pdf.

Preqin. (2018). *Private Equity & Venture Capital Spotlight.*, *14*(2). Accessed January 5, 2019. http://mandaportal.com/getattachment/ 9e7e42f3-f566-4b26-9834-f5dd456e6683/Preqin-Private-Equity---Venture-Capital-Spotli-(1).

Preqin. (2018a). *Preqin Quarterly Update: Private Equity &Venture Capital Q2 2018.* www.preqin.com.

Preqin. (2018b). *Gobal Private Equity Report.* Accessed January 5, 2019http://docs.preqin.com/reports/2018-Preqin-Global-Private-Equity-Report-Sample-Pages.pdf.

Probitas Partners. (2004). *Private Equity Market Environment.* Report. Accessed October 25, 2009. http://www.circlepeakcapital.com/press/probitas_market_overview.pdf.

Rifkin, James. (2011). *The Third Industrial Revolution: How Lateral Power Is Transforming Energy, the Economy, and the World.* Palgrave Macmillan.

Rochon, Louis-Phillipe. & Rossi, Sergio. (Eds.) (2015). *The Encyclopedia of Central Banking*, Edward Elgar.

Rochon, Louis-Phillipe. & Rossi, Sergio. (2013). "Endogenous Money: the Evolutionary Versus Revolutionary Views." *Review of Keynesian Economics, 1* (2), 210–229.

Samuelson, Robert. J. (2007). "The Private Equity Boom." *The Washington Post*, March 15.

Rosenberg, Emily. (1982). *Spreading the American Dream: American Economic and Cultural Expansion, 1890 – 1945.* New York: Hill and Wang.

Saunders, A. (1994). *Financial Institutions Management: A Modern Perspective.* Burr Ridge, IL: Richard D. Irwin.

Saunders, A. & Cornett, M. (2002). *Financial Institutions Management: A Risk Management Approach.* Columbus: McGraw-Hill College.

SEC. (2014). *Spreading Sunshine in Private Equity.* Report. www.sec.org.

Seccareccia, M. (2012). "Financialisation and the transformation of commercial banking; understanding the recent Canadian experience before and during the international financial crisis." *Journal of Post Keynesian Economics, 35* (2), 277-300.

Scholes, L., Wright, M., Westhead, P. & Bruining, H. O. (2009). "Family-Firm Buyouts, Private Equity, and Strategic Change." *Journal of Private Equity, 12* (2), p. 7-18.

Scholes, L. & Meuleman, M. (2010). Assessing the impact of private equity on industrial relations in Europe. *Human Relations, 63*(9), 1343-1370.

Shapiro, R. & Pham, N. (2008). *American Jobs and the Impact of Private Equity Transactions.* Research Report, USA: SONECON.

Smith, A. J. (1990). "Corporate ownership structure and performance: the case of management buyouts.' *Journal of Financial Economics, 27* (1).

Sprague, Jeb. & Ietto-Gillies, Grazia. (2014). "Transnational corporations in twenty-first century capitalism: An interview with Grazia Ietto-Gillies." *Critical Perspectives on International Business*, 10(1/2), 35-50

Standing, Guy. (2011). *The Precariat: The New Dangerous Class*. Bloomsbury Academic.

Statista. (2019). "The world's 50 largest companies based on number of employees in 2017." *The Statistics Portal*. Accessed Jmauary 10, 2019. https://www.statista.com/statistics/264671/top-20-companies-based-on-number-of-employees/.

Stiglitz, Joseph. (2012). *The Price of Inequality: How Today's Divided Society Endangers Our Future*. Norton.

Stockhammer, Engelbert. (2004). "Financialisation and the slowdown of accumulation." *Cambridge Journal of Economics*, 28(5), 719–741.

Stockhammer, Engelbert. (2009). "The finance-dominated growth regime, distribution, and the present crisis." *Department of Economics Working Papers* wuwp, *127*, Vienna University of Economics and Business, Department of Economics.

Tannon, J. M. & Johnson, R. (2005). "Transatlantic Private Equity: Beyond a Trillion Dollar Force." *Journal of Private Equity*, 8 (3), 77-80.

Tate, A. (2007). *The Effect of Private Equity Takeovers on Corporate Social Responsibility*. International Officer, Australian Council of Trade Unions. Accessed October 10, 2009. http://www.accsr.com.au /pdf/pet_speech_Alison_Tate.pdf.

Taub, Stephen. (2007). "*Record Year for Private Equity Fundraising*". *CFO.com*, January 11.

Taymoigne, É. (2010). *Minsky's two-price theory of investment: uncertainty, financial structure, and arbitrage between new and existing capital assets*, Minsky's Summer School, US. Accessed November 20, 2015. http://www.levyinstitute.org/pubs/conf_june10/ Tymoigne_Two _Price.pdf.

The Economist. (2011). "*The great unknown. Can policymakers fill the gaps in their knowledge about the financial system?*" Jan 13th.

Jni Global Union. (2008). *Pension Fund Investment in Private Equity*. Report.

Varoufakis, Yanis. (2013). *The Global Minotaur: America, Europe and the Future of the Global Economy*, New York: Zed Books.

Veblen, Thornstein. [1899 (2008)]. *The Theory of the Leisure Class*, online at www.gutenberg.org.

Weidig, Tom. & Mathonet, Pierre-Yves. (2004). *"The Risk Profile of Private Equity"*. *Working Paper Series*. Accessed November 10, 2012. http://ssrn.com/abstract=495482.

Wheatley, J. (2010). "Capital markets: Private equity funds explore the market." *Financial Times*. Accessed August 10, 2011. http://www.ft.com/cms/s/0/cbfe7ce6-571c-11df-aaff- 0144feab49a.html# axzz1 ezwgqbFE.

Wilpert, B. (2009). "Impacts ofglobalisation on human work." *Safety Science*, *47*(6), 727-732. https://doi.org/10.1016/j.ssci.2008.01.014.

Wray, L. R. & Tymoigne, É. (2008). *"Macroeconomics Meets Hyman P. Minsky: The Financial Theory of Investment."* *Working Paper*, *543*, Kansas City: The Levy Economics Institute and University of Missouri. Accessed November 25, 2015. http://core.ac.uk/download/ pdf/63664 63.pdf.

Wrigth, M., Jensen, M., Cumming, D. J. & Siegel, D. (2007). "The impact of private equity: setting the record straight." *Corporate Financier*, *94*.

Weil, D. (2014). *The Fissured Workplace: Why Work Became So Bad for So Many and What Can Be Done to Improve It*, Boston: Harvard University Press.

On Pension Funds

Bradford, Hazel. (2018). "Unions look for jobs to go with their infrastructure investments." *Pensions & Investments*. Accessed December 10, 2018. https://www.pionline.com/article/ 20180430/ PRINT/180439980/ unions-look-for-jobs-to-go-with-their-infrastructure-investments.

Ivashina, V. & Lerner, J. (2018). *"Looking for Alternatives: Pension Investments around the World, 2008 to 2017."* Harvard University and NBER, First draft: August 24.

Kaul, I., Conceição, P., Le Goulven, K. & Mendoza, R. (Eds.). (2003). *Providing public global goods: managing globalisation*. New York: Oxford University Press.

Madi, Maria A. Caporale. (2018). "Pension Funds' Challenges after the 2008 Global Crisis: Key Problems for Future Generations." *Open Journal of Economocs and Finance*, 2, 117-125.

OECD. (2008). *Pension Markets in Focus*, December – Issue 5, OECD Publishing. Accessed March 20, 2016. http://www.oecd.org/finance/private-pensions/41770561.pdf.

OECD. (2014). *"Mortality Assumptions and Longevity Risk: Implications for pension funds and annuity providers."* OECD Publishing.

OECD. (2018). *Pension Funds in Focus*. OECD Publishing. Accessed December 20, 2018. http://www.oecd.org/pensions/private-pensions/pensionmarketsinfocus.htm.

Pietras, J. (2009). "Austerity Measures in the EU: A Country by Country Table." In *Special G-20 Issue on Financial Reform*. Accessed June 20, 2010. http://www.europeaninstitute.org/Special-G-20-Issue-on-Financial-Reform/austerity-measures-in-the-eu.html.

PwC. (2014). *"Asset Management 2020: A brave new world."* Report. Accessed May 25, 2015. http://www.pwc.com/us/en/press-releases/2014/pwc-global-assets-under-management.jhtml.

Skerrett, K., Roberts, C., Weststar, J. & Archer, S. (Eds.). (2018). *The Contradictions of Pension Fund Capitalism*. New York: Cornell University Press.

Uni Global Union. (2008). *"Pension Fund Investment in Private Equity."* Report. UNI.

On Pragmatism and Ethics

Brasset, J. & Holmes, C. (2016). "Building Resilient Finance? Uncertainty, complexity, and resistance." *The British Journal of Politics and International Relations*, *18*(2), 370–388.

Houser, Nathan. (2010). Reconsidering Peirce's Relevance. In *Ideas in Action: Proceedings of the Applying Peirce Conference* edited by M. Bergman, S. Pavola, A-V. Peitarien and H. Rydenfelt Nordic Studies in Pragmatism 1. Helsinki: Nordic Pragmatism Netword.

Houser, Nathan. (2015). "The Imperative for Non-Rational Belief." *Cognitio.*, *16*(2), 273-289.

Houser, Nathan. (2016). "Semiotics and Philosophy." *Cognitio.*, *17*(2), 313-336.

Houser, Nathan. (2016a). "Social Minds and the Fixation of Belief" In *Consensus on Peirce's Concept of Habit* edited by Donna West and Myrdene Anderson.

Ibri, Ivo. A. (2017). *Kósmos Noetós: The Metaphysical Architecture of Charles S. Peirce.* Springer.

Ibri, Ivo. A. (2002). "Considerações Sobre O Estatuto Da Ética No Pragmatismo De Charles S. Peirce." *Síntese, Rev. De Filosofia, 29* (93), 117-123.

Ibri, Ivo. A. (2004). "Semiótica e Pragmatismo: Interfaces Teóricas." *Cognitio.*, *5* (2), 168-179.

Ibri, Ivo. A. (2017a). "The Double Face of Habits. Time and Timeless in Pragmatic Experience." *Rivista di Storia dellla Filosofia, 3*, pp. 455-474.

Lane, R. (2004). "On Peirce's early realism" *Transactions of the Charles Sanders Peirce Society, 40* (4), 575-605.

Peirce, Charles. S. (1965/1931). *Collected Papers of Charles Sanders Peirce.* Hartshorne, P. Weiss y A. W. Burks (Eds.), Cambridge, MA: Harvard University Press (Cited as CP).

Peirce, Charles. S. (1992-98). *The Essential Peirce: Selected Philosophical Writings.* Vol. *1* (1867-1893), ed. by N. Houser & C.J.W. Kloesel 1992, vol. *2* (1893-1913) ed. by the Peirce Edition Project 1998. Bloomington & Indianapolis: Indiana University Press. (Cited as EP).

On the Commons and Climate Finance

Ge, Jing. & De Clercq of Djavan. (2017). *"The road to sustainability"*. Tsing Capital White paper. Tsing Capital Strategy & Research Center.

IEA. (2015). *World Energy Outlook*. Accessed June 20, 2016. http://www. iea.org/publications/freepublications/publication/WEO2015SpecialRep ortonEnergyandClimateChange.pdf.

Intergovernmental Panel on Climate Change. IPCC. (2014). *Fifth Assessment Synthesis Report*. Accessed March 10, 2015. ww.ipcc.ch/ pdf/assessmentreport/ar5/.../SYR _AR5 _LONGER REPORT.pdf.

Madi, Maria A. Caporale., Kennet, Miriam. & Windham-Bellord, Karen A. (Eds.). (2017). *Value, Valuation, Valuing*. UK: Green Economics Institute.

Madi, Maria A. Caporale. (2017). "New Business Models in the Energy Sector." *Science Journal of Energy Engineering.*, 5 (3), 63-67.

Makovich, L. (2012). *Putting Energy Back to Work*. Accessed July 10, 2014. http://www3.weforum.org/docs/WEF_EN_EnergyEconomic Growth_IndustryAgenda_2012.pdf.

McCrone, A. (2016). "If interest rates turn, clean energy will find it tougher.*" Bloomberg New Energy Finance*.

Metz, B., Davidson, O., Swart, O. & Pan, J. (2001*). Climate Change 2001: Mitigation*. IPCC WG III contributions to TAR, Cambridge: Cambridge University Press.

Okoh, A I. S. (2014). "Post-Kyoto Protocol Negotiations: Sunrise or Sunset for Economic Growth in Africa?" *Journal of Good Governance and Sustainable Development in Africa, 2* (3).

Ostrom, Elinor. (1990). *Governing the Commons: The Evolution of Institutions for Collective Action*. Cambridge: Cambridge University Press.

UNFCC. (2016). *Summary and recommendations by the Standing Committee on Finance on the 2016 biennial assessment and overview of climate finance flows*. UNFCCC Standing Committee on Finance. Accessed March 10, 2017. http://unfccc.int/files/cooperation_and_

support/financial_mechanism/standing_committee/application/pdf/201 6_ba_summary_and_recommendations.pdf.

UNFCC. (2016a). *Biennial Assessment and Overview of Climate Finance Flows Report.* UNFCCC Standing Committee on Finance. Accessed March 10, 2017. http://unfccc.int/files/cooperation_and_support/ financial_mechanism/standing_committee/application/pdf/2016_ba_te chnical_report.pdf.

Welsh, M. (2014). "Resilience and Responsibility: governing uncertainty in a complex world." *Research Paper.* Department of Geography and Earth Sciences, Aberystwyth University.

ABOUT THE AUTHOR

Maria Alejandra Madi
PhD in Economics, Professor at UNICAMP, Brazil,

Maria Alejandra C. Madi holds a PhD in Economics and a MA in
Philosophy. Her academic career includes a long-term professorship at
UNICAMP and visiting professorships at the University of Manitoba and
Kassel. In addition to her research interest on the financial challenges of
globalisation, her line of investigation includes the philosophy of science at

the Center for Pragmatism Studies (Brazil). She is currently member of the board of the Green Economics Institute (UK), Chair of the World Economics Association Online Conference Program (UK), Editor of the WEA Books Conference Series and of the WEA Pedagogy Blog. She co-edited some of The Green Economics Institute books, including *The Greening of Global Finance* and *Values, Valuation and Valuing*. She also co-edited some of the World Economics Association books: *Ideas towards a new international financial architecture?* and *Capital and Justice*. Her latest authored books include *Small Business in Brazil: competitive global challenges* and *Pluralist Readings in Economics: key-concepts and policy-tools for the 21st century*. Her latest co-authored book is *Introducing a New Economics: Pluralist, Sustainable and Progressive*. She is also Assistant Editor of the *International Journal of Pluralism and Economics Education* and Co-editor-in-Chief of *The Open Journal of Economics and Finance*.

INDEX

H

habits, ix, 27, 28, 29, 30, 33, 114, 140, 144, 145, 164
hedge funds, 3, 15, 22, 43, 53, 106

I

India, 99, 100, 101, 104, 122, 157
industry, vii, ix, x, 7, 8, 11, 12, 13, 14, 17, 25, 28, 37, 38, 39, 40, 45, 48, 49, 56, 57, 60, 62, 64, 65, 66, 70, 83, 84, 86, 87, 88, 91, 93, 96, 99, 101, 106, 112, 119, 128, 130, 134, 136, 140, 141, 142, 143, 145, 148, 154, 159
inequality, x, 13, 33, 34, 76, 81, 134, 138, 141, 155, 161
information, iv, 22, 57, 58, 62, 63, 65, 69, 70, 71, 79, 89, 102, 106, 107, 115, 117, 142, 151
initial public offering (IPO), 40, 58, 63, 64, 99, 103
innovation, 12, 41, 69, 75, 120, 130, 135, 142, 143
institutional investors, vii, ix, 20, 22, 23, 40, 42, 43, 56, 60, 98, 111, 116, 124, 125, 127
insurance companies, 16, 22, 25, 43, 54, 68, 98
interest rates, 42, 50, 52, 59, 92, 165
investment, v, vii, ix, x, 3, 4, 6, 8, 9, 10, 11, 13, 14, 16, 17, 19, 20, 21, 22, 23, 34, 39, 42, 43, 44, 45, 47, 48, 49, 50, 51, 54, 55, 56, 57, 58, 59, 61, 62, 64, 67, 69, 78, 80, 83, 84, 85, 86, 87, 89, 91, 95, 97, 98, 100, 101, 102, 104, 105, 106, 111, 113, 114,116, 122, 123, 124, 125, 127, 128, 129, 130, 135, 136, 138, 141, 142, 143, 144, 151, 153, 156, 161, 162, 163
investment banks, 3, 43, 44, 105, 125
investment vehicles, 45, 69

J

jobs, 21, 74, 75, 76, 78, 79, 80, 81, 87, 133, 141, 143, 147, 148, 151, 160, 162

K

knowledge, 28, 75, 142, 143, 161

L

labour, v, ix, 4, 7, 9, 10, 13, 21, 22, 24, 26, 34, 47, 51, 73, 74, 75, 76, 77, 78, 79, 80, 82, 83, 84, 85, 86, 87, 112, 117, 133, 134, 138, 141, 147, 148, 152, 153, 154, 155, 158
legislation, 11, 107
leveraged buy-outs, 80
limited partners, 12, 15, 16, 22, 26, 27, 67, 68, 69, 107
liquidity, 3, 4, 8, 10, 14, 22, 23, 26, 42, 43, 44, 46, 48, 50, 53, 55, 59, 60, 61, 91, 93, 117, 119
loans, 40, 42, 43, 44, 46, 124, 126

M

management, vii, viii, x, 3, 4, 7, 9, 11, 12, 13, 16, 20, 34, 39, 41, 43, 44, 45, 46, 48, 49, 50, 52, 53, 55, 58, 59, 61, 63, 64, 65, 66, 67, 68, 69, 70, 71, 72, 79, 81, 89, 91, 92, 93, 96, 97, 99, 100, 102, 104, 113, 114, 115, 116, 119, 120, 127, 128, 136, 137, 139, 141, 143, 147, 149, 150, 151, 154, 156, 160, 163
manufacturing, 6, 10, 70, 74, 75, 81, 123
marketing, 22, 106, 118, 120
markets, x, 4, 5, 7, 8, 9, 10, 13, 19, 21, 22, 23, 26, 40, 41, 42, 44, 45, 46, 51, 53, 55, 56, 58, 61, 62, 63, 64, 66, 67, 73, 74, 77,

Related Nova Publications

STRATEGIC VALUE MANAGEMENT: A DYNAMIC PERSPECTIVE

EDITOR: Marek Jabłoński

SERIES: Business Issues, Competition and Entrepreneurship

BOOK DESCRIPTION: This book is intended for management theoreticians and business practitioners interested in effective value-based management in a dynamically changing environment. It can also be an inspiration for business consultants in terms of the implementation of the modern concepts of value-based management in modern companies.

HARDCOVER ISBN: 978-1-53614-089-7
RETAIL PRICE: $230

A COMPREHENSIVE INVESTIGATION ON EXECUTIVE-EMPLOYEE PAY GAP OF CHINESE ENTERPRISES: ANTECEDENTS AND CONSEQUENCES

AUTHOR: Changzheng Zhang

SERIES: Business Issues, Competition and Entrepreneurship

BOOK DESCRIPTION: The executive-employee compensation gap, a newly focused dimension of the executive compensation packages by the previous literature, has been given a great deal of attention because of the growing inequality in the compensation practices within the firms over the past two decades in China.

HARDCOVER ISBN: 978-1-53612-813-0
RETAIL PRICE: $270

TRUST, TRUSTWORTHINESS, AND STEWARDSHIP: A TRANSFORMATIVE APPROACH

AUTHORS: Cam Caldwell, Ph.D. and Verl Anderson, DBA

SERIES: Business Issues, Competition and Entrepreneurship

BOOK DESCRIPTION: This new book identifies insights about the ethical issues associated with trust and trustworthiness, and their relationship to the leader's obligations as an ethical steward.

HARDCOVER ISBN: 978-1-53615-093-3
RETAIL PRICE: $195

CORPORATE SOCIAL RESPONSIBILITY OF SOCIAL ECONOMY ENTERPRISES

EDITORS: Candido Roman-Cervantes and Olga Gonzalez-Morales

SERIES: Business Issues, Competition and Entrepreneurship

BOOK DESCRIPTION: The authors of this book intend to show and interest the reader to a rigorous and varying panorama of the state of research applied to social economy companies and how they integrate CSR into their objectives.

HARDCOVER ISBN: 978-1-53614-176-4
RETAIL PRICE: $160

To see complete list of Nova publications, please visit our website at www.novapublishers.com